BERENICE ABBOTT

PHOTOGRAPHER

BERENICE ABBOTT

PHOTOGRAPHER

AN
INDEPENDENT
VISION

G EORGE S ULLIVAN

CLARION BOOKS
New York

Clarion Books
a Houghton Mifflin Company imprint
215 Park Avenue South, New York, NY 10003
Copyright © 2006 by George Sullivan

The text was set in 13-point Galliard.

www.houghtonmifflinbooks.com

Printed in the U.S.A.

Library of Congress Cataloging-in-Publication Data

Sullivan, George, 1927–
Berenice Abbott, photographer : an independent vision / by George Sullivan.
p. cm.
Includes bibliographical references and index.
ISBN-13: 978-0-618-44026-9
ISBN-10: 0-618-44026-7
1. Abbott, Berenice, 1898–1991—Juvenile literature. 2. Photographers—United States
—Biography—Juvenile literature. 3. Women photographers—United States—
Biography—Juvenile literature. I. Title: Independent vision. II. Title.
TR140.A25S85 2006
770.92—dc22

2005030736

VB 10 9 8 7 6 5 4 3 2 1

Contents

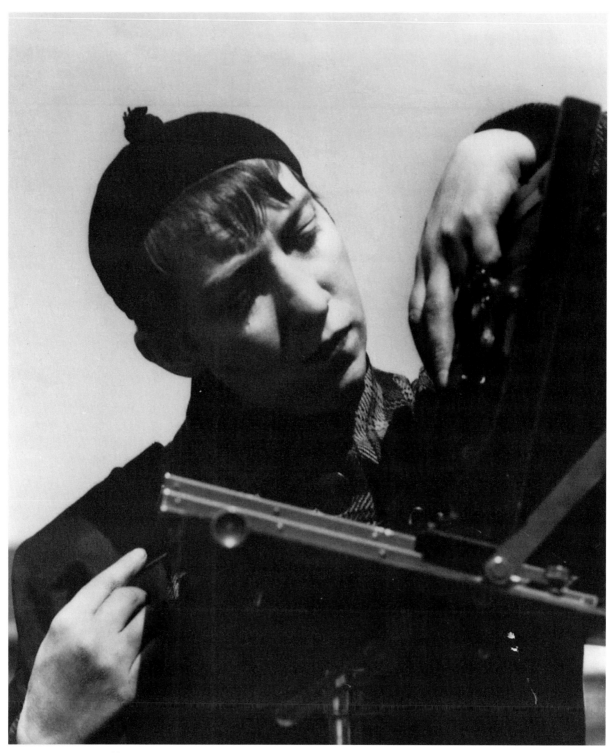

Berenice Abbott at work, 1938. (Commerce Graphics Ltd., Inc., Consuelo Kanaga)

INTRODUCTION

During the Depression-plagued years of the 1930s, she became a familiar sight to countless New Yorkers: a short, slim, serious-faced young woman with close-cropped hair, wearing trousers and a tailored jacket. The curious watched as she hovered over her bulky camera on its metal tripod, carefully adjusting its height, then composing the image on its glass screen, her head shrouded beneath a dark focusing cloth. With a craving to see things as they really are, she targeted her lens on the city's towering skyscrapers, its little shops and markets, the townhouses of Greenwich Village, and immigrant neighborhoods of the Lower East Side.

There was nothing new about taking pictures of New York. Photographers had made the city their subject from the camera's earliest days. But Berenice Abbott's carefully composed, sharply focused photographs of the city are as fresh and full of energy today as when she made them three-quarter of a century ago. One critic called her accomplishment "the finest record ever made of an American city."

Berenice's precise and straightforward images had an important impact on American culture. She was one of a generation of Americans who broke free of the past to introduce new forms and styles in art, architecture, music, and literature. Her crisp, clean, realistic photographs, a true expression of the modern movement, helped to break new ground. To *The New York Times*, Berenice Abbott was "a pioneer of modern American photography."

While it is for her New York photographs that she is best remembered, they represent only one aspect of her long and richly honored career. Earlier, living in Paris, Abbott won acclaim for her stunning portrait photographs. She later mastered scientific photography; her pictures of magnetic fields and objects in motion succeeded in making clear scientific principles of great complexity. At the same time, her work was hailed for its photographic beauty.

Berenice Abbott was also a teacher, writer, inventor, and historian. She was an archivist, too, helping to preserve the work of Jean Eugène Atget (aht-ZHAY), a French master photographer. She struggled for years to win for Atget the recognition he deserved.

When Berenice Abbott was making her splendid photographs of New York in the 1930s, the world of photography was very different from what it is today. Picture magazines were just beginning to flourish. Art galleries devoted to photography were nearly nonexistent, and museums that included photography in their collections were a great rarity. To the art world, photography was a hobby, like stamp collecting or quilt making, and not to be taken very seriously.

This was true despite the work of many earlier and greatly talented individuals who, like Eugène Atget, pioneered in taking "factual" pictures. During the Civil War, Mathew Brady organized teams of photographers and sent them out to cover battle sites. William Henry Jackson and several other cameramen provided

For this striking view of New York's financial district, Abbott took her camera to the top of a sixty-seven-story skyscraper, then aimed the lens downward. Taking the photograph through the building's rooftop grillwork added drama to the scene.
(COMMERCE GRAPHICS LTD., INC.)

scenic views of the American West in the years after that war.

Near the turn of the last century, two urban photographers, Jacob Riis and Lewis Hine, used their pictures as tools of social reform. Riis, a Danish immigrant, exposed the brutal living conditions of New York slum dwellers. Hine photographed young children working in factories. Such work became known as "documentary photography."

When it came to taking pictures of their own, most Americans of the 1930s used small boxy cameras to produce informal, quickly made images—that is, snapshots. This casual attitude toward photography started forming in the late 1880s, when George Eastman introduced the Kodak camera. Until then, taking photographs was a complicated process, involving cameras that required loading an individual glass plate coated with chemicals for each picture taken.

The Kodak offered a compact roll of paper-backed film (with the photosensitive chemicals coated on the paper). The camera was easy to use and inexpensive. In his advertising Eastman told people to take photographs on vacations, on holidays, and at the "Christmas house party." He introduced the idea of the family photo album. Use the camera, he said, to document your lives and record your memories. He said that no home should be without one. Eastman mass-produced Kodak cameras, and millions of people bought them.

A small group of photographers, known as "pictorialists," looked upon snapshot photographers with dismay. Pictorialists wanted their work to be regarded as an art form, like painting or sculpture. They sought picturesque effects with their photographs, often focusing on wet or snow-covered streets or drizzly

American writer Janet Flanner was on her way to a costume party when she arrived at Abbott's Paris studio, which explains the top hat on which she had strung two masks. (COMMERCE GRAPHICS LTD., INC.)

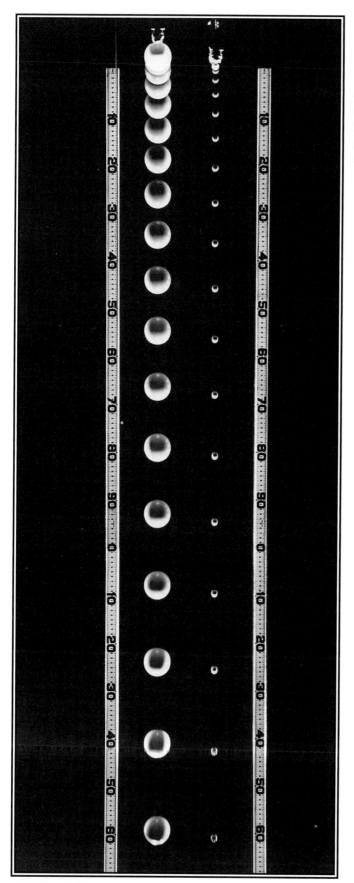

Many of Abbott's photographs taken during the 1960s illustrated scientific principles. This multiple-exposure image shows that balls of unequal size fall at exactly the same rate of speed. (COMMERCE GRAPHICS LTD., INC.)

landscapes. They also favored a soft-focus technique, which produced blurriness, or they altered their images by hand to make their photographs look like paintings.

When someone mentioned pictorialism to Abbott, her blue eyes narrowed and a frown clouded her face. She deplored the "prettiness" of pictorialism. Photography, Abbott said, is meant "to communicate the realities of life, the facts which are to be seen everywhere about us." She called pictorialists "precious" and "exclusive."

Although Abbott sometimes yielded to a streak of shyness, she never made any secret of her views about photography. As a result, she often clashed with highly regarded figures in the art world, including Alfred Stieglitz, who was a photographer, art dealer, editor, and publisher. Stieglitz had the foresight to realize that one day photography would rank as a major cultural force, affecting every aspect of the way in which the world learned or communicated. But to Abbott, Stieglitz was no more than the leader of an "advanced or super-pictorialist school." Throughout her career she skirmished with Stieglitz and his followers.

Berenice Abbott was never a follower. She realized, of course, that her need to lead an independent life and speak out, to buck the system, sometimes caused setbacks in her career.

Abbott lived out her final years in Maine, a feisty champion of photographic realism to the end. She died in 1991 at the age of ninety-three. By that time her superb Paris portraits, her strong and eloquent images of New York, and her remarkable scientific photographs had earned her a reputation as one of the greatest and most influential American photographers of the twentieth century. When an exhibition of her photographs opened at the Museum of Modern Art in New York in 1970, displaying exam-

Pictorialists often tried to make their photographs look like paintings. This example, of light reflections in a New York park at night, was taken by Alfred Stieglitz in 1895 or 1896, when Stieglitz was a champion of pictorialism. (LIBRARY OF CONGRESS)

ples of work from her long career, *The New York Times* hailed her for her "special artistry" and "extraordinary eye [and] flawless technique." A "master photographer," the paper called her. Abbott could take pleasure in the fact that she had achieved that status very much on her own, avoiding popular trends and always remaining true to her vision. Berenice Abbott followed her own script.

SPIRIT OF A REBEL

Berenice Abbott was the youngest of four children, two boys and two girls. Except for occasional references to her twice-divorced mother, a schoolteacher at the time of her first marriage, Berenice seldom spoke of what were her painful early years. "The last thing in the world I like to talk about is my childhood," she told James McQuaid and David Tait, who interviewed her in some depth in July 1975. Others who questioned Berenice were told much the same. Even her closest friends knew little about the years when she was growing up.

She was born in Springfield, Ohio, on July 17, 1898, and named Bernice (with no middle "e"). Two months before her second birthday her father filed for divorce, charging Berenice's mother with adultery. The court ruled that Berenice's two brothers, Earl Stanley Abbott and Frank Abbott, would remain with their father. Berenice and her twelve-year-old sister, Hazel Abbott, were to be raised by their mother.

A few years after the divorce, Berenice's mother married a second time. Berenice received this news from a relative. "I was about five when I was at my aunt's place down below Chillicothe [Ohio], and my aunt or cousin came in and said, 'Oh, Berenice, you have a new papa.'"

Her mother's remarriage didn't make life in the Abbott family any easier. "I don't really like to talk about it" was all Berenice would say on the topic, although she did once describe her step-father as "just a madman."

After Berenice's mother divorced a second time, she moved the family frequently, first to Cincinnati, then Columbus, and finally Cleveland. Berenice's two brothers rejoined the family there. Her sister, meanwhile, rushed into an early marriage. "I think [it was] to get away from home," said Berenice.

In families ripped apart by conflict, the children often pay a high price. With Berenice, however, the family turbulence seemed to have had a positive effect, strengthening her character. "I got hard pretty early" is the way she put it. What she endured made Berenice realize that she could not depend on adults for affection and guidance. She understood that she would have to be completely self-reliant and prepared to control her own destiny. She became, as she once described herself, "a very independent kid."

Her mother's difficult life also caused Berenice to form harsh opinions about men and marriage. "Marriage is the finish for women who want to do their work," Berenice said. "It's good only for men. You can't let things hold you back. And when they're married, women let everything hold them back. Most marriages are tragedies for ambitious women."

Berenice finished grade school and went on to Cleveland's Lincoln High School, taking college preparatory courses. She liked school and wanted to learn, and she loved sports, especially tennis and swimming. But she was shy in the classroom. She felt uncomfortable raising her hand or speaking before a group. However, this was a problem she figured she could do something

In the years before World War I, Abbott attended Cleveland's Lincoln High School, where she was a good student. (CLEVELAND PUBLIC LIBRARY, PHOTOGRAPH COLLECTION)

about, although she didn't quite know what. She certainly didn't intend to let her shyness interfere with the plans she had for going to college.

Berenice's career aspirations in high school varied widely. For a while she thought she might like to become a farmer or an astronomer. She also wanted to fly, to become a pilot. By the time she graduated, she had settled on journalism as a career.

Berenice graduated from Lincoln High School in January 1917, a time of great turbulence in America. In April the United States entered World War I. While most of the war's savage fighting took place in Europe, and United States troops were actively involved for only about eight months, the war helped to bring about remarkable changes in American cultural life. Many of these directly affected women, who had long been barred by cus-

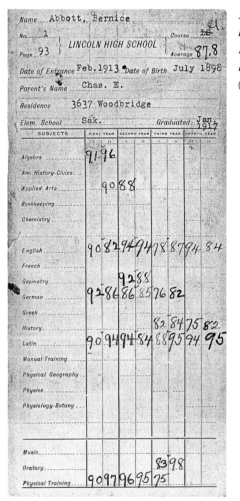

Abbott excelled in a number of subjects in high school, including Latin and algebra. She earned her highest mark in oratory—despite a problem with shyness.
(CLEVELAND MUNICIPAL SCHOOL DISTRICT)

tom and law from seeking careers in many professions. Previously, teaching, nursing, and library work were looked upon as the vocations most suitable for women. Berenice was well aware of this. But once the war began, much of the male working force was drawn into the army and navy. Women were then able to move into many jobs from which they had once been excluded and hold them at least until the war ended.

There were important social changes, too. While most people of the time believed a woman's role in life was to bear and raise children, and largely remain in the home, some women felt they could adopt a more liberated style of life. They could smoke, drink, wear makeup, and attend lively parties.

Berenice could not help but be caught up in the changes that were taking place. Hardly had she received her diploma than she exhibited her independent spirit with what she referred to as her "first act of rebellion." She bobbed her hair.

"The day after I graduated from Lincoln High School in Cleveland, Ohio, I had the barber cut off the long, thick braid which hung down my back," Berenice said, "and with its departure came a great sense of relief. I felt lighter and freer."

Getting one's hair bobbed was a serious matter. Bobbing your hair meant that you were thumbing your nose at the established order. You were a rebel. Girls and women who bobbed their hair usually powdered their noses, rouged their cheeks, used eye shadow, and wore short skirts. They went out dancing and often smoked in public. Berenice *loved* to dance. The turkey trot, bunny hug, grizzly bear, "shaking the shimmy," and other dances of the time were considered "indecent" by many and sent shock waves through the middle classes. Berenice smoked, too, and made no effort to be secretive about it. She smoked openly, whenever she felt like it.

The "new" Berenice entered Ohio State University in Columbus in February 1917, enrolling as a journalism student. Being shy, she was filled with anxiety about fitting in and making new friends. To her great surprise, she created a sensation. "My bobbed hair startled the campus," she said. "A handful of students from New York at once mistook me for a 'sophisticate,' a worldly New Yorker. All of this because of my short hair. We became friends, and a new life began for me."

Berenice's college friends included Susan Jenkins, an outstanding student who was in Berenice's English class, and James Light, who helped to edit the campus literary magazine. Sue and Jimmy were an important influence on Berenice, introducing her to books and ideas that helped to open the world to her.

Sue helped to make Berenice aware that a change was taking place. "I think there is something I should tell you," she said to Berenice one day.

"Well, that's up to you," Berenice replied.

"Jimmy and I are living together," Sue said.

Berenice's brow wrinkled. She didn't quite know what Sue meant by "living together."

Several days later Berenice happened to be visiting Sue's apartment. She saw Jimmy's clothing everywhere. His shaving gear was in the bathroom. Berenice suddenly realized what "living together" meant.

When Berenice returned to Ohio State for the fall semester, she found that the war had brought about some changes. Male students were being trained to become officers in the armed forces, and the campus was dominated by the ROTC (Reserve Officers' Training Corps). Also, with coal in short supply, classrooms were often unheated, and classes were canceled for days at a time as a result.

Another side effect of the war involved a literature class she planned to take. Since journalism was her chief interest, she felt a literary background would be helpful to her. But the professor who was to conduct the class, whom Berenice deeply respected, was dismissed because Germany was an enemy nation and the professor happened to be German. "[A] lot of stupidity flourishes with any war," Berenice observed.

With American men serving in the armed forces during World War I, many new job opportunities became available for women. Here, students at Central High School in Washington, D.C., get training in auto mechanics. Note that all the girls pictured are wearing their hair bobbed. (LIBRARY OF CONGRESS)

To add to her frustration, she was required to take courses in which she had little interest. History courses, for instance. "I just thought history was the dullest thing on earth," she recalled. Science was also a bore, she decided. Later in her career, after she had devoted a decade to taking a series of advanced scientific photographs, she looked back and saw that she had been foolish. Those science courses could have been valuable to her if only she had paid attention.

Perhaps Berenice's biggest disappointment was that Sue Jenkins and Jimmy Light did not return to school. They had left Columbus and gone to New York City to live.

Berenice missed her friends terribly. Then one day she received a letter from Sue saying that she and Jimmy were planning on getting married. Jimmy had gotten a job as a director at the famous Provincetown Playhouse. They were living in a large apartment in Greenwich Village and invited Berenice to join them, although they warned her that she would probably have to sleep on a mattress on the floor. Sue even offered to send Berenice the twenty dollars she would need for train fare from Columbus.

The letter started Berenice's mind churning. She thought about her situation and decided there was little reason to remain at Ohio State. But she felt certain her mother didn't want her running off to New York, and she was right. When Berenice told her mother her plans, the two quarreled. "I think what she wanted me to do was to stay in Cleveland and marry somebody and be around there," Berenice said. "And that was the last thing in the world that I wanted to do."

"It wasn't easy," said Berenice of her latest act of defiance, "and I didn't like leaving my mother, but it was either my life or hers."

A view of the campus of Ohio State University in 1917, Abbott's freshman year.
She dropped out of college early the following year. (OHIO STATE UNIVERSITY ARCHIVES)

And the "pull" of New York, as she described it, was very strong. She was a nineteen-year-old girl trying to decide who she was. But she was sure of one thing: The thought of living the same kind of life that everyone else was living stifled her. She wanted to be with people who, in mind and spirit, at least, were free and independent. She wanted to be with people like herself.

In a letter to Sue, Berenice asked her to send the fare. Soon the money arrived. In February 1918, Berenice, with a mixture of eagerness and anxiety, packed her bags and boarded a train in Cleveland bound for New York City.

The difficulty of Berenice's early years, and the sense of independence she developed as a result, caused a ripple effect throughout her entire life. Those years toughened her.

Much later, after she had become famous, the New York Public Library presented an extraordinary exhibition of Berenice's work, a well-chosen selection of almost two hundred photographs, as well as her books, inventions, and more. The show received glowing reviews nearly everywhere. One critic, however, writing for a New York newspaper, found the exhibition to be "unsettling." He said, "[N]o single clue to her personal history has been allowed in this survey." None of Berenice's intimate relationships was mentioned, said the critic. No insights into Abbott, the person, were given.

That is exactly the way Berenice wanted it, of course. Perhaps because of her painful childhood, she appeared to be closed off from her emotions and rejected anything that might be construed as sentimental. She was a very private person. Berenice's photographs were never about Berenice. She used the camera to produce clear, concise, straightforward records of people and places. What was personal remained invisible.

THE VILLAGE

On a cold and snowy January night in New York City in 1917, several shadowy figures approached Washington Square Arch, the tall and stately monument at the northern edge of Manhattan's Washington Square Park, which is looked upon by many as the gateway to Greenwich Village, a neighborhood south of Fourteenth Street. Led by Marcel Duchamp, a French artist well known for his radical forms of painting and drawing, the group carried lanterns, sandwiches, bottles of wine, cap pistols, and red, white, and blue balloons.

Without a word they slipped through a doorway at the base of the arch, climbed the iron staircase, lifted the trapdoor, and scrambled out onto the arch's wide, flat top. There they made a fire in a bean pot, passed out the sandwiches and wine, and had a midnight picnic.

After dining and drinking, they turned to the business of the evening. They tied the balloons to the top of the arch, fired their cap pistols, and read a proclamation that stated that from that day forward Greenwich Village would be "an independent republic," and as such committed to "socialism, sex, poetry, conversation, dawn-greeting, anything—so long as it's taboo in the Middle West."

Abbott's photograph of Washington Square Park dates to the 1930s. The famed arch is at the center of the picture. (NEW YORK PUBLIC LIBRARY)

When Greenwich Villagers awoke the next morning to see the balloons waving in the wind and later heard what had taken place that night, they shrugged. It was merely another act of foolishness, the memory of which lasted only about as long as the balloons.

Freedom and independence were nothing new in Greenwich Village. The area had long attracted radicals, rebels, and creative people. Socialism, anarchism, pacifism, Freudianism, feminism, free love, and birth control were at home there.

To many young men and women who were dissatisfied with their middle-class lives in the small towns of the Midwest, Greenwich Village offered a life far more open than their own, and they sought it out.

Freedom and independence were just what Berenice was seeking on the February night in 1918 when she arrived in New York City. A fierce blizzard raged. She hurriedly made her way to the address Sue Jenkins had given her, a four-story Greenwich Village apartment house at 137 Macdougal Street, where she would be living.

When Berenice found Sue Jenkins and Jimmy Light, they and some friends were huddled in a small room trying to keep warm. Someone was reading aloud the popular poems of Edna St. Vincent Millay, then in her late twenties, whose verse was often taken as a voice of feminism. To escape the cold, it was suggested that the group go to their favorite hangout, a nearby bar called the Golden Swan, more commonly known as the Hell Hole. It was packed and noisy, with men and women clustered around small tables, talking, laughing, drinking, and smoking. Framed paintings lined the walls. The crowd included writers and artists but also longshoremen, politicians, prostitutes, and gangsters. The owner, Berenice was told, kept a pig in the basement.

Berenice, slim and shy, "the youngest thing around," as she described herself, was in awe. This was a wholly different world for her.

Some of the people whom Berenice met that night and in the days and weeks that followed would become her close friends. They provided her with companionship and support during her early years in New York.

For Abbott and her Greenwich Village friends, the Golden Swan, also known as the Hell Hole, was a chummy gathering place. Its character was captured by artist John Sloan in this early-twentieth-century etching. (NEW YORK PUBLIC LIBRARY)

One was Hippolyte Havel. Short, dark, with long hair and a walrus mustache, and decades older than Berenice, Havel was a self-described anarchist. To support himself, he toiled as a cook, waiter, and dishwasher at Polly's Restaurant, a popular meeting place for artists and writers on the ground floor of the building where Berenice and her friends lived.

Havel kiddingly announced at their first meeting, or shortly thereafter, that Berenice was his daughter. This news delighted Berenice. It meant she had a friend. "He was just what I needed," she said. "He sort of sheltered me."

Berenice was absolutely fascinated by the women she met. Many looked upon marriage and motherhood as options, not fate. Some had male partners; others were gay or bisexual. They allowed Berenice, who sometimes felt affection for members of her own sex, to be more comfortable about her own feelings.

As for her career plans, Berenice still clung to the idea of becoming a journalist. She thought she might enroll at Columbia University to study writing and editing. But visits to the Columbia campus in Upper Manhattan were a disappointment to her. It was too busy, too crowded. The place "seemed like a hell of a sausage factory," she said. She soon gave up the idea of going back to college.

For her food and rent money, "just to earn a buck," Berenice held an assortment of odd jobs. She worked in an office, waited tables, and even dyed hair in a beauty salon. She worked for a clipping service, cutting articles out of newspapers and magazines for clients who wanted to see coverage of particular topics. She called a job she had trying to collect past-due debts a "nightmare."

Berenice also became involved with the Provincetown Playhouse, which was next door a 133 Macdougal Street. The Provincetown Players was a theater company that had been formed a couple of years earlier by a group of summer residents in Provincetown, Massachusetts, on Cape Cod. Led by George "Jig" Cook, the members wrote their own plays and performed them in their homes. They later moved to an open-air theater that they created on a Provincetown wharf.

Their remarkable success led the Provincetown group to shift operations to New York City, where they rented a Greenwich Village theater. There they staged one-act productions, including a number of dramas by Eugene O'Neill, who was on his way to becoming one of America's greatest playwrights.

In a theater company that used candles for footlights, created decorative columns out of rolls of wrapping paper, and spread coats and blankets over kneeling volunteers to make them look

Abbott's first home in New York, at 137 Macdougal Street. Her apartment was above Polly's Restaurant, which had become the Open Door by 1936, when this photograph was taken. The Provincetown Playhouse was next door, at number 133. (NEW YORK PUBLIC LIBRARY)

like boulders, there was plenty for Berenice to do. A high point in her theatrical career came when she was offered a minor part in an O'Neill play titled *The Moon of the Caribbees.*

Berenice quickly accepted the role, partly because she thought it might help her to overcome her shyness. "This will get you over it," she thought. "This will put some punch in you."

The play was a success. It was one of a series of the playwright's one-act seagoing dramas, and critics found it powerful and moving, feeling it displayed touches of the genius O'Neill would later display in his full-length works.

As she was embarking on her new career, Berenice, with Sue Jenkins, Jimmy Light, and several of their friends, moved from Macdougal Street to a rambling old seventeen-room apartment building called the Clemenceau, also deep in Greenwich Village. Each person had his or her own room at a "very cheap rent," as Berenice noted.

Not long after the move, Berenice's acting career came to an abrupt end. While rehearsing for a part in a second O'Neill play, she came down with influenza, a particularly virulent strain known as the Spanish flu. By 1918 the disease had become a global disaster, killing tens of millions of people. In New York City, the Health Department reported that some 10 percent of the population had the Spanish flu.

The disease struck Berenice with such savagery that she had to be taken by stretcher from her room at the Clemenceau to nearby St. Vincent's Hospital. There she remained for weeks, sometimes hovering between life and death. When she was well enough to be released, she was still so weak that she found it difficult to walk.

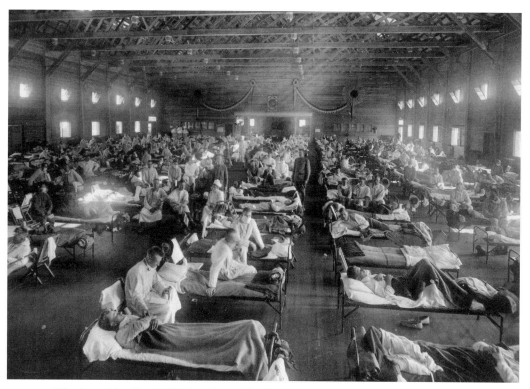

The flu epidemic of 1918 is estimated to have killed at least twenty million people worldwide. Here, flu victims crowd an emergency hospital at Camp Funston at Fort Riley, Kansas. (WIDE WORLD)

When Berenice's mother learned of her daughter's illness, she got in touch with her sister's son, Guy Morgan, who lived in well-to-do circumstances in Westchester County, just north of New York City. The family was happy to have Berenice as a guest and did what they could to make her comfortable. But she didn't like staying with the Morgans. She felt her cousin and his family were overly concerned with their material possessions and too intent on conforming to all the accepted standards of taste and conduct. "Dirty bourgeois" is what her friend Hippolyte would call them, she said to herself. She was glad when she felt well enough to leave.

During the many weeks that she spent recovering, Berenice had time to think seriously about her life in New York, which seemed to be without any direction. She didn't know quite what to do, but she knew she needed to make a change. She eventually made up her mind to become a sculptor. She liked the idea of making objects out of clay, though she realized that she had no great passion for the art. But sculpting, as she herself put it, would at least serve as kind of an anchor for her.

Berenice also decided that she had to move out of the Clemenceau and find an apartment that offered more privacy. Berenice wanted freedom, but at the Clemenceau there was too much of it.

"There were a lot of kids just sounding off, really," she recalled, "very immature people. God knows, I was immature myself, but they were, too, and there was a lot of silly stuff going on."

Berenice found a small two-room apartment not far from the Clemenceau in "Clothesline Alley," a narrow street between two rows of houses off Christopher Street near Sixth Avenue. It had earned its nickname from the laundry that residents strung up over the street to dry. One room of her apartment was for sleeping; the other she used as a studio for sculpting. Now on her own, and better able to think, reflect, and apply herself, she plunged into her new career.

Through her interest in sculpting, Berenice made several new friends, among them the French artist Marcel Duchamp, who had come to New York from Paris several years earlier. Charming and witty, Duchamp was a Dadaist, one of a group of artists and writers who rejected the accepted ideas of art, thought, and morality, and often expressed their views through outrageous art and behavior. Duchamp had been the leader of the small group that had climbed to the top of the Washington Square Arch in January 1917 to declare Greenwich Village "an independent republic."

Dadaists would take commonplace objects and present them as works of art. Duchamp himself had created enormous controversy in 1917 when he had submitted a porcelain urinal turned upside down as his entry in an art exhibition. (In 2000 the urinal, which had become a revered piece of sculpture by then sold for $1.75 million.) He had also exhibited his *Mona Lisa,* a reproduction of Leonardo da Vinci's famous painting, to which Duchamp added a mustache and goatee. He later would become active in the creation of the "Société anonyme," one of the first museums devoted entirely to modern art.

When Berenice met Duchamp, he was in his mid-thirties and was spending much of his leisure time playing chess. Although he was skilled enough to compete on a championship level, he often played Dada-style chess, which permitted only moves that were illegal.

Duchamp encouraged Berenice in her sculpture. He even asked her to create a set of chess pieces for him.

It was through Duchamp that Berenice met Man Ray, an artist who was to play an important role in her life. Man Ray was a painter, sculptor, poet, and essayist who had recently taught himself the basics of photography and was using his camera to document his art. In his long and sometimes stormy career, Man Ray would make lasting contributions as a photographer, and also as a painter, sculptor, and filmmaker.

Man Ray had been introduced to Dadaism by Duchamp, and

French artist Marcel Duchamp, whose innovative ideas influenced a generation of painters and sculptors, encouraged Abbott in her ambition to become a sculptor. (CORBIS/PHOTOGRAPH BY CARL VAN VECHTEN)

the two were planning to bring out a magazine titled *New York Dada*. When the magazine was finally published, however, it quickly proved a failure. Man Ray became deeply depressed as a result. He moved to Paris in 1921.

Looking back, Berenice observed that the people who interested her the most were usually eccentric, or, as she described them, people who were "far out" or had "weird values." And she also realized that this "was a form of rebellion against the Midwest and everything it stood for and all the values people had."

Despite her many colorful friends, Berenice remained her

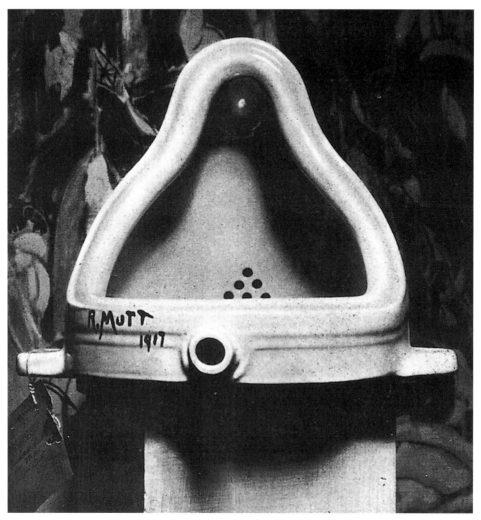

The Fountain, *Marcel Duchamp's entry for a 1917 art exhibition in New York. Instead of using his own name, Duchamp signed the urinal "R. Mutt."*
(MARCEL DUCHAMP; PHOTOGRAPHED BY ALFRED STIEGLITZ, PHILADELPHIA MUSEUM OF ART: THE LOUISE AND WALTER ARENSBERG COLLECTION, 1950)

quiet, independent self. Ralph Steiner, like Berenice a Midwesterner and later notable as a photographer, remembered her. "I used to meet her at parties," he recalled. "She was kind of shy, but she looked kind of forbidding, and the lady who dressed mannishly was always sort of guarding her."

The "lady who dressed mannishly" was Elsa von Freytag-Loringhoven, whom everyone called the Baroness. She was the widow of a titled German businessman who had come to New York almost twenty years earlier. After his death, the Baroness earned a living as an artists' model and by working part-time in a cigarette factory. She also sculpted and wrote poetry.

By the time Berenice met her, Baroness Elsa was a woman in her mid-forties and very well known in artistic and literary circles. Her prominence was due in large part to her eccentric dress. Every day around five or six o'clock, the Baroness walked her leashed dogs through Washington Square Park. She wore a short-sleeved, waist-length, open jacket; a tartan kilt, and a battered fur coat. To this she attached bottle caps, tiny dolls, and small stuffed birds. Sometimes she wore a birthday cake on her head. In summer she would drape a necklace over her shoulders from which she hung a bird cage with a live canary. She made earrings from tea bags. She preferred black lipstick and coated her cheeks with yellow face powder, and she often had her head half shaved and painted bright purple.

Baroness Elsa, a Dadaist like Duchamp and Man Ray, intended such costumes to be a form of art. Her other creations included pieces of sculpture made from discarded objects such as trash cans and old automobile tires. Poetry was the field in which she showed a special talent. Indeed, some Village residents considered her to be an accomplished poet. Berenice was one of her most avid admirers. "When she read her poems, she was magnificent," Berenice remarked. "I sincerely believed her to be a great artist." Berenice also liked the Baroness for her liberated view of life and willingness to indulge in "every whim and fancy."

Young Village artists sought out Baroness Elsa for her advice. "She criticized their work honestly," said Berenice, "though sometimes brutally." At the time, Berenice was beginning her career as a sculptor, and the Baroness cheered her efforts.

The Baroness also urged Berenice to think about leaving New York to live in Paris. Thousands of poets, artists, writers, musicians, and others who had come to reject what they saw as Americans' preoccupation with material comforts had crossed the Atlantic after the world war ended in November 1918. They had settled in the French capital, then considered the cultural center of the Western world.

The idea appealed to Berenice, who was often disheartened by the commercialism that seemed to surround her. A man who made a lot of money was judged to be more important and held in higher esteem than one who made little. Berenice couldn't accept this.

While money wasn't important to her, she knew she needed it. But how could she earn a living? She had no interest in any of the few professions then open to women. So she resigned herself to being poor. And she figured she could be poor in Paris just as easily as in New York.

She could continue to work on her sculpting in Paris. While there, she hoped, she might be to be able to join other students in classes offered by Antoine Bourdelle, a famous French sculptor and painter.

As Berenice began making preparations for her departure for Paris, one of her friends had some stern advice for her. The friend was a free-thinking poet named Sadakichi Hartmann. Then in his fifties, Hartmann was the son of a wealthy German father and a

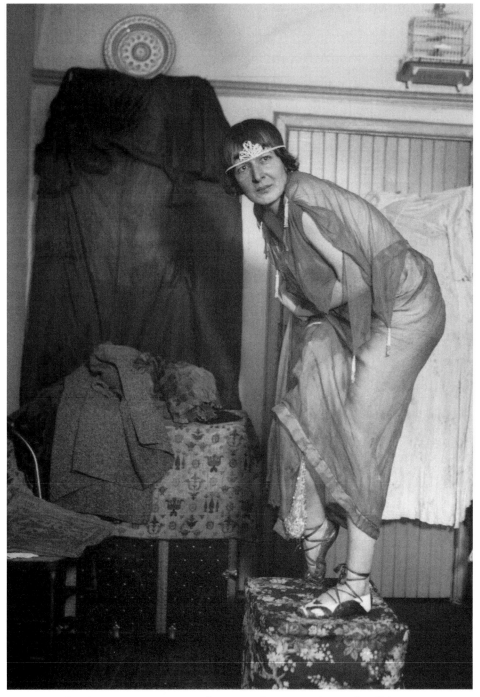

Baroness Elsa, here posing for art students, was known for her outlandish costumes, although this one was less bizarre than most. (CORBIS)

came from modeling for artists and sculptors. One was John Storrs, a modernist sculptor from Chicago whom she had met on the *Rochambeau*. Berenice also taught American-style dancing, and occasionally she sold small pieces of her sculpted work. Storrs bought a figure of a woman in a hoop skirt. An English couple purchased some figurines. "Somehow, fantastically enough, I always survived," she said.

As she had planned before leaving New York, Berenice sought to take classes in sculpture under Antoine Bourdelle, but she found them too expensive. Instead, she began attending drawing classes, which were affordable for her.

Since she had only a meager knowledge of French, the friends she made were largely American and British. Tommy Earp, a would-be poet who was British, showed her the sights of Paris. "He was wealthy," Berenice remembered. "And we would go out in the evening, and we'd spend a fortune. And the next day I would maybe not have enough to eat."

Not long after her arrival in Paris, Berenice was reunited with Marcel Duchamp and Man Ray. Duchamp was living in Montparnasse, a section of Paris on the Left Bank of the Seine that was home to a thriving art community. Artists Francis Picabia and Fernand Léger and poets Jean Cocteau and Ezra Pound all lived within a stone's throw of Duchamp.

In the afternoons and evenings, Montparnasse offered a lively outdoor café life. La Rotonde and Le Select were among the cafés that Berenice and her friends frequented. Smaller cafés were to be found on side streets. Berenice hailed the ability of the French to enjoy themselves "as one of the most valuable attributes of the French civilization."

A painter, sculptor, and filmmaker, Man Ray moved in 1921 from New York to Paris, where he made his living as a portrait and fashion photographer. He hired Abbott as his assistant in 1923. (LIBRARY OF CONGRESS/PHOTOGRAPH BY CARL VAN VECHTEN)

Man Ray had set up a studio in his hotel room and started taking portrait photographs, drawing his subjects from the community of Paris writers and artists. His portraits were good, but what created an absolute sensation were the photographs that he was producing by an unusual process. He would take common objects, such as pocket combs, bunches of keys, or the contents of his medicine cabinet, and place them directly on a piece of light-sensitive photographic paper; he would then direct a flash of

When she finally reached Paris, she was penniless and her future looked bleak. Then her fortune changed.

One evening not long afterward, she and Man Ray visited Le Boeuf sur le Toit, one of their favorite nightclubs. The two friends quickly brought each other up to date. Berenice recounted her recent unrewarding stay in Berlin. Man Ray, on the other hand, had only good news to report. Now highly acclaimed as a portrait photographer, he found his career was soaring. He had opened a new studio to replace the cramped hotel room where he had once both lived and worked. His clients included not only the best known of Paris' writers and artists but also travelers from other parts of Europe as well as America.

But Man Ray had a problem. "My last assistant," he said, "knew too much. He got in my way." Man Ray had fired the assistant, and now he was looking for someone to take his place, someone he could train.

"My brain clicked at that moment," Berenice recalled. "What about me?" she asked.

"Well, why not?" replied Man Ray. "Do you want to come in tomorrow morning? I'll give you fifteen francs [about three dollars] a day."

Having a steady job and being dependent on someone besides herself for her income was a new experience for Berenice. The situation made her feel uncomfortable. But she realized the alternative was being penniless and perhaps even homeless. "Sister," Berenice said to herself, "you have to make this go!" She took on her new job with determination and enthusiasm.

Man Ray gave her instruction in darkroom work. He began by showing her how to mix the necessary chemicals. He showed her

The lively sidewalk cafés of Paris provided the settings for artists and writers to meet and exchange ideas and support each other's work. (LIBRARY OF CONGRESS)

how to develop the exposed film by treating it with chemical solutions to produce a negative. He taught her how to make a photographic print by directing light through the negative onto specially treated paper, and how to "fix" the print in chemical baths once the developing and printing stages had been completed.

From the beginning, Berenice was deeply serious in her approach to the work. No details were skipped. She repeatedly checked the temperatures of the solutions with which she was working. She shifted the prints from one tray to another with the greatest care; there was no dripping or spilling of solutions.

Berenice's training and experience in drawing and sculpture helped her. She sought to get a three-dimensional quality into Man Ray's portraits so as to make them as lifelike as possible. "Man Ray was amazed that I made such good prints in such a short time," Berenice said. He was happy to increase her salary.

One day, after Berenice had been working as his darkroom assistant for more than a year, Man Ray suggested that instead of getting another raise, she use his equipment during her lunch hour to earn extra money taking portrait photographs of her own. Berenice agreed. She then began asking friends to stop by to pose for her. "The first [portraits] I took came out well, which surprised me," Berenice recalled. "I had no idea of becoming a photographer, but the pictures kept coming out and most of them were good." She decided to start charging for her work

Before long, her little business was flourishing. Some weeks she paid Man Ray more for film, chemicals, photographic paper, and other supplies than he was paying her in salary.

Not only did Abbott's roster of clients grow in number but they increased in renown as well. They included André Gide; the poet, actor, and playwright Jean Cocteau; the painter and designer Marie Laurencin; and Janet Flanner, a novelist who worked as the Paris correspondent for *The New Yorker*.

It was Cocteau who suggested to Berenice (who was still Bernice) that she make a change in her first name, adding another "e." She liked the idea. She kept repeating the new name to herself: *"Behr-e-nees . . . Behr-e-nees."* She thought it sounded much better. She was Berenice for the rest of her life.

Berenice's reputation as a portrait photographer eventually began to match that of Man Ray. The two were becoming competitors. A split seemed inevitable.

Man Ray's pleasingly pretty portrait of Berenice Abbott, made in 1925.
(THE J. PAUL GETTY COLLECTION)

One day a wealthy American art collector named Peggy Guggenheim, who often lent her financial support to the Paris colony of artists and writers, telephoned Man Ray to arrange a studio appointment to have her portrait taken, not by Man Ray himself but by Berenice. Afterward, Man Ray was livid. He now realized that Berenice had become a serious business rival. By the next day Abbott was out of a job.

Berenice immediately made plans to establish a studio of her own. But she had mixed feelings about what she was going to do. "He changed my whole life," Berenice said about Man Ray. "He was the only person I ever worked for, and I was extremely grateful to have the job, to have the opportunity to learn." Unfortunately, their relationship was coming to an unpleasant end.

Friends of Berenice's stepped forward to help her. When she made arrangements to purchase a view camera—a camera that exposed one photograph at a time on a 4" x 5" negative, from which prints were made—Peggy Guggenheim lent her the money to pay for it. As partial repayment, Berenice later photographed Peggy's children. Robert McAlmon, another wealthy American, along with his wife, the single-named writer Bryher, also lent Berenice money, which she used to outfit her darkroom.

As a portrait photographer, Abbott had no wish to imitate Man Ray. She developed a different style, avoiding anything contrived or fanciful. As a result, Berenice's portraits were quite unlike Man Ray's. "His portraits of men were good, but he always made women look like pretty objects," Berenice once said. "He never let them be strong characters in themselves."

Evidence of this is a portrait that Man Ray made of Berenice during the time that she worked as his darkroom assistant.

Berenice was a handsome young woman, serious and determined. Man Ray, however, showed her as being pretty and precious. That was not Berenice.

Berenice felt that a portrait should be much more than a likeness. It should reveal the subject's character. Facial expression, dress and surroundings, gesture or mannerism—all of these were to work toward imparting some idea of the person's inner life.

Berenice worked carefully and thoughtfully, devoting a full day to each portrait session. She never tried to schedule several portrait sittings in a single day in order to increase her income.

"To photograph a person there must be an exchange—a cooperation," said Abbott. "The 'sitting' is more like a visit and sometimes we would get into a lively conversation."

Sometimes, Abbott would take several shots without any film in the camera at the beginning of a sitting, a fact she didn't reveal to the subject. She did so to get the sitter to loosen up. Once the person was relaxed, "I was ready to do something," Abbott said.

In her ambition to achieve this sense of realism in her portraits, it is likely Berenice was influenced by the work of the French photographer Nadar. Born Gaspard-Félix Tournachon in 1820, Nadar, who once identified himself as "a photographer for the time being," was also a journalist, novelist, critic, caricaturist, and hot-air balloonist. But it is for his brilliant portrait photographs that he is remembered.

In his portraits, Nadar sought to capture the essential ingredients of the subject's personality. "[The portraits] sum up a temperament in a single glance, and give us a whole attitude toward experience in a grimace, a smile or a look of defiance," critic Hilton Kramer noted.

In the spring of 1926 a Paris gallery presented a collection of Berenice's portraits in what was the first exhibition devoted to her work exclusively. The show ran for two weeks. It was well attended, and her work attracted the attention of Paris critics.

One hailed Berenice for her distinctive style, for the strength, sincerity, and simplicity of her portraits. "There is absolutely no

"Portraits can be the real revelation of the person," Abbott said. Her portrait of André Gide reveals the French writer's elegance as well as his reserve.
(Commerce Graphics Ltd., Inc.)

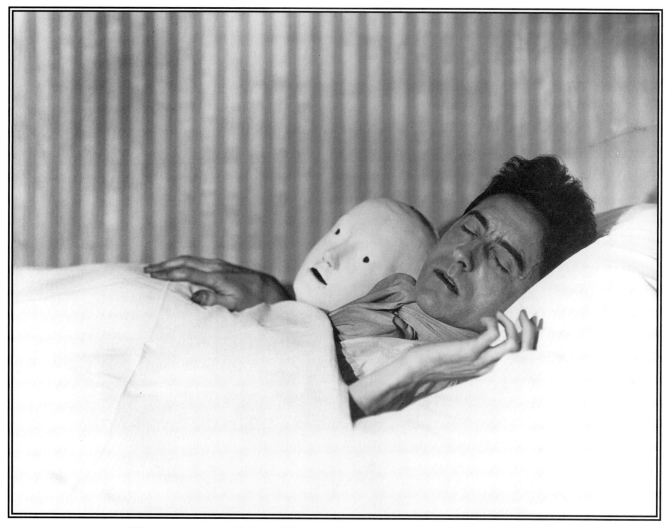

When poet, actor, and playwright Jean Cocteau appeared at Abbott's Paris studio to have a portrait photograph taken, he brought a mask with him and suggested this reclining pose. (COMMERCE GRAPHICS LTD., INC.)

striving for an 'effect' or a 'pretty picture,'" noted the *New York Herald of Paris.* "There are no elaborate backgrounds to detract from the personality of the sitter, no trick lighting effects or unnecessary retouching." This honest and open approach would stamp Abbott's work throughout her long career.

"A Magical Record"

One day in 1925, while Berenice was still working as Man Ray's assistant, he showed her several pictures of Paris architecture and street life that had been taken by an elderly and little-known French photographer. The photographs dazzled her. She would later describe them as "the most beautiful photographs ever made."

The photographs were the work of sixty-eight-year-old Eugène Atget. They were to open a new world for Abbott and play an important role in her life for the next forty years.

Atget's thousands of photographs documented every aspect of life in Paris from 1890 through the early 1920s, creating a dramatic true-life archive. *The New York Times* would later refer to the collection as "a magical record."

For decades Atget had scraped out a living by selling prints of his photographs to Paris painters and sculptors who were looking for subject matter for their work. The renowned French impressionist Maurice Utrillo, who drew and painted landscapes and street views common to the Montmartre section of Paris, had copied scores of his scenes from photographs that he had purchased from Atget for a few francs. Degas, the impressionist renowned for his paintings and drawings of ballerinas and racehorses, did the same. A painting by Degas that depicts ladies'

Atget preferred to take photographs in the early-morning hours, when his subjects—the streets, the parks, and public monuments—were empty of people. (LIBRARY OF CONGRESS)

hats in a shop window is very similar to an Atget photograph.

After Berenice left Man Ray and set up her own studio, she visited Atget, trudging up the stairs to his fifth-floor apartment. On the door was a hand-lettered sign that read: DOCUMENTS POUR ARTISTES—"documents for artists."

Berenice described the Atget she met that day as "slightly stooped . . . tired, sad, remote, appealing." He wore old and patched clothes. He seemed to live entirely for his work, his photography.

The old man showed Berenice some of the albums in which he had mounted his prints—forthright and uncluttered images of Parisian parks, empty streets, shop windows, bridges, trees, cafés, courtyards, and street vendors.

"The subjects were not sensational, but shocking in their very familiarity," Berenice noted. "The real world, with wonderment and surprise, was mirrored in each print." Berenice picked out and purchased as many prints as she could afford. She asked Atget to put others aside for her until she could pay for them.

Berenice returned many times to visit Atget. He explained some of the difficulties he had had in hauling his forty-pound camera through the streets of Paris. Photographers were uncommon at the last turn of the century. People were suspicious of him. Some even thought he might be a spy.

Berenice later persuaded Atget to visit her studio and sit for his portrait. To her surprise, Atget arrived in a handsome overcoat. "I had always seen him in patched work clothes," Berenice said. "It would have been desirable to photograph him in these, too, since they were exquisitely photogenic."

Berenice took three different poses—a side view and a front view with Atget seated, and a version with Atget standing. They clearly show Atget's weariness and dampened spirit.

Several days later, Abbott went to show Atget the photographs she had taken. When she arrived at his apartment door, she noticed the little DOCUMENTS POUR ARTISTES sign was missing. Her knock went unanswered. When she sought out the building manager, he told her that Atget had died. Berenice was shocked and saddened.

In the days that followed, Berenice feared that Atget's photographs might be lost forever if she did not act. She began making an effort to buy the entire collection. After almost a year of discussion with André Calmette, Atget's best friend and the person he had named to carry out his wishes, Berenice, with financial help from friends, was successful in purchasing the collection. It consisted of eight thousand original prints and almost fifteen hundred glass plates. (Despite such technological advances as the development of roll film, many professional photographers continued using glass plates well into the 1900s.)

To preserve the glass plates, Berenice and an assistant cleaned each one and placed it in a glassine envelope. They then numbered and classified them all. The work took months.

When Berenice finally returned to her studio and her portrait work, Atget and the enormous collection of prints and negatives that she had acquired were seldom far from her thoughts. In the years that followed, she took on the task of establishing Atget's rightful rank as a great photographer—and she succeeded. Atget is today recognized as having been a serious influence on many important photographers—among them Walker Evans, known for his images of Depression-era America and the American landscape in general, and, of course, Abbott herself. Collectors, dealers, and art museums covet Atget's work. But as Berenice noted, it took two lives to build Atget's reputation—"his and mine."

Meanwhile, Berenice's portrait business was flourishing. Her list of clients now included some of the most prominent Parisians and Americans living in Paris. She photographed the novelists James Joyce, Janet Flanner, Djuna Barnes, and André Maurois, and the poet Claude McKay. Artists Max Ernst, Thelma Wood, and Gwen Le Gallienne posed for her, as did

In her photograph of Eugène Atget, Abbott showed his slumping shoulders to reflect his weariness from, as she put it, "thirty years of lugging around his bulky view camera and heavy glass plates." (Commerce Graphics Ltd., Inc.)

The clarity and simplicity of Atget's work was an inspiration not only to Abbott but also to countless other photographers who favored a documentary style.
(LIBRARY OF CONGRESS)

socially prominent figures like Peggy Guggenheim and Dorothy Whitney.

Many of Abbott's subjects felt that they were confirming or perhaps even boosting their social status by being photographed by her. Sylvia Beach, an American who operated an English-language bookshop that had become a popular meeting place for Paris' English-speaking art community, described Abbott and Man Ray as "the official portraitists of 'the Crowd'"—those in vogue, in style, the socially elite. To be "done" by either of them meant that you rated as somebody, said Beach.

Abbott photographed the Irish writer James Joyce at his Paris home. Severe eye problems, which led to near blindness, were the reason Joyce wore an eye patch. (COMMERCE GRAPHICS LTD., INC.)

As the decade of the twenties was drawing to a close, the reputation of Berenice's work continued to grow, and critics began to take note of her realistic style. In 1928 she was one of a group of photographers invited to display examples of their work at a Paris theater in what was called the First Salon of Indepen-

dent Photographers. Hungarian-born street photographer André Kertész, who had photographed the Hungarian Revolution in 1918, Nadar, Man Ray, and Atget were among those included. To the organizer of the show, these photographers offered images that were "exact, clean, precise."

In the photographs that she exhibited, Abbott demonstrated the ability to capture her subjects while they were in deep thought or involved in spontaneous action. As one critic noted, Abbott "knows perfectly how to let go of her emotions to present her characters according to their own actions."

The thirty-one-year-old Abbott could rejoice in her success. It was not merely that her portrait work was winning universal praise. For the first time in her memory, her financial problems had melted away. Her income came not only from the fees paid to her by her clients—she had made a rule very early in her career never to take a photograph without charging for it—but also from selling prints of her portraits to magazines and book publishers. Photo agencies, companies that provided prints to a wide variety of clients, also wanted her portraits.

Although she was enjoying fame and financial security, Berenice was not entirely content. She had been reading about America and was feeling wistful about her native country. The idea of returning home was beginning to appeal to her.

When she told her Paris friends what she was thinking, they thought she was crazy. She had made a comfortable and fulfilling life for herself here. Why change? Berenice fully realized how much she had attained in a relatively short span of time and that she might be putting everything at risk by going back to Amer-

This Abbott photo of Djuna Barnes, a major literary figure of the time and a friend of Abbott's, was taken in Paris in 1926. Abbott later photographed Barnes in New York. (COMMERCE GRAPHICS LTD., INC.)

ica. Nevertheless, she felt "an extremely strong pull" to return.

In January 1929, after nearly eight years in Europe, Abbott boarded the ocean liner *Homeric,* bound for New York. She told her friends it would be a six-week visit.

Berenice wasn't going back to the United States merely as an American longing for home. There were some very practical reasons for the trip. One of her goals was to find an American firm willing to publish a book devoted to the photographs of Eugène Atget. She had already gotten a Paris publisher, Henri Jonquières, interested in the idea. But he would produce the book only on condition that Berenice find an American distributor for an English edition.

Berenice was also interested in doing some photography. Not portrait photographs, however. Before her departure, Abbott had gotten in touch with several Paris magazine editors and publishers asking them whether there might be "any particular subject that interested them." Some said they might be able to use views of New York. Before leaving Paris, Berenice bought a small lightweight camera, a Kurt Benzin Primarflex, to photograph New York street scenes.

For several weeks during February and March 1929, Berenice prowled Manhattan, uptown and downtown, from east to west, taking photographs that she hoped she might be able to sell to her European clients. She had been away from New York for almost eight years and was startled by the changes that had taken place. New York was in the midst of an extraordinary building

Originally from New Jersey, Sylvia Beach settled in Paris and in 1919 founded Shakespeare and Company, a lending library and bookshop that became a literary center for Americans living in the city. Abbott made this portrait of her in 1926. (COMMERCE GRAPHICS LTD., INC.)

boom, with towering skyscrapers rising in great clusters in midtown and in the financial district downtown.

Near Grand Central Terminal it seemed that every nineteenth-century building was being leveled, to be replaced by soaring structures of forty stories or more. Farther uptown workers were drilling deep into the bedrock, laying the foundation for what would be Rockefeller Center. These projects would soon transform the city's skyline.

Berenice was excited by what was happening. "The American scene just fascinated me," she said in an interview years later. "I was like a stranger. I could have been from Mars almost. When you're very fresh, impressionable, sensitive, and you are away for years, and then you come back and you see this whole strange land and it's your own . . . it fascinates."

Berenice's enthusiasm soon led her to think seriously about moving back to New York. It was a hard decision to make. It meant giving up the many friends she had made in Paris. It also meant abandoning her flourishing portrait business.

Nevertheless, Berenice had faith in her ability to thrive in New York. She felt that the lessons she had learned in Paris could be applied to her new life, and that she could succeed as a portrait artist in New York as she had done in Paris.

But it was her plan for photographing the city that energized her. In later years, as a teacher, Berenice always had one piece of advice for novice photographers. "Find a worthy subject," she would say. "It has to be something that excites your imagination to the extent that you are forced to take the picture." Berenice now had a worthy subject of her own. She would do for New York what Eugène Atget had done for Paris.

A page from Abbott's album in which she displayed her early New York photographs. These images are of the city's financial district.
(Metropolitan Museum of New York)

Following her return to Paris in April 1929, she stayed only long enough to sell some of the New York photographs she had taken for European magazines. She also traded or sold her furniture and just about everything else she owned—except the Atget photographs and negatives. These she had packed up and shipped to New York. They filled twenty crates.

5

A NEW BEGINNING

A few weeks after her arrival in New York, Berenice rented an apartment at the stylish Hotel des Artistes on Sixty-seventh Street, just west of Central Park. It had wonderful natural light, ideal for studio portraits. She began purchasing the equipment she needed for her studio and a darkroom.

While Berenice was in high spirits about New York and her plans to photograph the city, there were some aspects of her life in France that she missed. In New York there was really nothing to compare to the Paris café life, and she often recalled how she and her friends would gather in the evening after work and exchange information and ideas.

And whereas in Paris she felt her role as a photographer was commonly accepted, in New York things were different. Homemaking and motherhood were still considered to be women's chief responsibilities. In many professions, including photography, women were seldom to be seen.

Berenice understood that to be successful she would have to demonstrate a level of skill and talent well beyond that of her

Abbott in a self-portrait made in 1932. (NATIONAL PORTRAIT GALLERY)

male counterparts. "I realized from very early days that the cards were stacked against women and that things are more difficult for them," she said. "My mother even told me that. But I don't think I realized until pretty late just how deep it was. . . . It's a very profound prejudice that permeates everything without you being aware of it." She admitted there were times when she was disheartened and discouraged by the situation.

Prejudice wasn't her only problem. Once Berenice had returned to New York and begun to build a new life for herself, events began unfolding on a national scale that would also undermine her chance for success. A dramatic plunge in stock market prices in October 1929 triggered the Great Depression. The economy went into a tailspin. Millions of people were thrown out of work. The nation's banking system collapsed.

The Depression hit Berenice hard. By early 1930, she was almost penniless. Desperate, she turned to the only worthwhile property she owned besides her cameras—the Atget photos. She agreed to sell an interest in the Atget collection to Julien Levy, a New York art dealer, for one thousand dollars. Under the terms of the contract they both signed, Abbott would make prints of the photographs from Atget's glass plates, and Levy would sell them in a gallery that he planned to open in New York.

The arrangement never worked. When Levy found he was unable to sell Atget's images, or anyone else's, he lost interest in photography and devoted himself to selling paintings and sculpture. His interest, said Berenice, "went out the window."

Along with Julien Levy and the nose-diving economy, another problem faced Berenice: Alfred Stieglitz, regarded by many as the messiah of American photography. Abbott had not been in New

York for very long before she decided to visit Stieglitz. In his efforts to improve the way photographs were reproduced in periodicals and presented at exhibitions, and in his lifelong mission to have photography recognized as an art form, Stieglitz had deeply influenced the medium. His body of work stretched from the 1880s to the 1930s and included some of the most notable images ever made, among them a photograph depicting the hands of his wife, the artist Georgia O'Keeffe.

Abbott had never met Stieglitz and had never seen any of his photographs. She knew him only by reputation. While she was interested in seeing the work he had on exhibit, she also wanted to speak to him about Atget, with the idea of encouraging him to sponsor a show of the French photographer's work.

As a photographer and editor, Alfred Stieglitz exerted an enormous influence on twentieth-century photography and art. Abbott, however, had no admiration for him or his work.
(LIBRARY OF CONGRESS/PHOTOGRAPH BY CARL VAN VECHTEN)

Abbott went to meet Stieglitz at his gallery on Park Avenue in New York, where he was showing the work of several painters and photographers. One of them was Paul Strand, a young photographer whom Stieglitz championed. Strand had recently produced graceful close-up images of plants, rocks, driftwood, and forest scenes.

When they were together in the gallery, Stieglitz proudly showed Abbott a series of cloud and sky photographs that he had taken. He called them "Equivalents." Said Stieglitz, "I have a vision of life and I try to find equivalents for it in the form of photographs."

Abbott's brow wrinkled. She thought Stieglitz's cloud and sky photographs were dull.

Something else troubled her. While Stieglitz had some positive things to say about the work of Paul Strand, he also found fault with it. Was this any way to treat a protégé?

When Abbott mentioned Atget, Stieglitz showed some interest. But as far as Abbott was concerned, it didn't matter what he thought. She had already made up her mind. She would never permit Stieglitz to exhibit Atget's photographs. She was afraid he might openly criticize Atget's work as he had Paul Strand's. Abbott could not allow that to happen.

In the days that followed, Abbott thought she might have misjudged Stieglitz's photographs. Perhaps they were not boring. But when she went to see another show of his, she found only a handful of images to be worthwhile; most, she felt, were lifeless.

The truth was that Stieglitz didn't like Bernice and she didn't like him. In the years that followed, the unpleasant feelings that Abbott and Stieglitz had for each other did her no good. Stieglitz

Not long after her return to New York, Abbott became acquainted with Walker Evans, pictured here in 1937. Evans played a key role in the development of American documentary photography. Both he and Abbott made preliminary photographs of the city at about the same time, although they worked apart from each other. (LIBRARY OF CONGRESS/PHOTOGRAPH BY EDWIN LOCKE)

and his followers were the leaders of the museum world. They treated Berenice as an outcast for decades.

Berenice accepted the situation. She had certain views and principles. She intended to stand by them, no matter what.

Berenice also came to know photographer Walker Evans not long after her return to New York, and this association proved more rewarding. Evans was just getting started in photography. He, like Abbott, had grown up in the Midwest, dropped out of college, and lived in Paris. Both were making exploratory photographs of the city, and Abbott recognized a similarity in their styles.

The two also shared a dislike for Alfred Stieglitz and what they considered artiness in photographs. When Evans showed Stieglitz some of his work, he reported that it was "disastrous on both sides. We didn't like each other . . . he had no time for me."

During the period of their acquaintance, Abbott showed Evans her collection of Atget photographs, which were to have an important influence on Evans's documentary approach to photography. During the 1930s, Evans made photographs of people in Cuba and photographed the Depression poor for the Farm Security Administration. After 1938, he turned to urban America for his subjects and photographed in the streets, in subways, and from moving train windows. In doing so, he established himself as one of the preeminent American photographers of the twentieth century.

From the time she arrived in New York, Berenice worked diligently to establish herself as a portrait photographer. She planned to charge as much as $75 or $80 for a portrait, but she quickly found that people were unwilling to pay that amount. And no wonder. During the Depression, a factory worker earned less than $20 in a week; a family doctor, about $60. A haircut cost 25 cents. And as Berenice discovered, a person could go to a department store and have a photographic portrait made for just a few dollars. Berenice was offering a luxury service when there was no demand for one.

What clients Berenice had were usually her friends. One was Edna St. Vincent Millay, whom Abbott had first met in New York in the 1920s. They had seen each other frequently in Paris and were now reunited in New York.

Abbott photographed Edna St. Vincent Millay in 1930,
after both had returned to New York from Paris.
(COMMERCE GRAPHICS LTD., INC.)

Margaret Bourke-White was not only a pioneering photojournalist but also one of the most celebrated photographers of the time. Her career stretched from the late 1920s to the mid-1950s. (LIBRARY OF CONGRESS/PHOTOGRAPH BY ALFRED EISENSTAEDT)

Berenice did realize one of her goals. She found an American publisher who was willing to bring out the book of Atget's photographs. While the venture was helpful in gaining recognition for Atget, it did not result in any income for her. "I never got a cent from it," she said.

To earn money, Berenice turned again to the magazine market. She occasionally sold some of her New York photographs to *Vanity Fair*, *The Saturday Evening Post*, and *The Saturday Review of Literature*. For *Fortune* magazine she made portraits of business leaders in their offices. But it was wholly unlike the portrait work in her Paris studio. She found the so-called "captains of industry" to be a self-important bunch. They needed to be flattered. They wanted to be made to look handsome and distinguished.

Berenice's work with *Fortune* also enabled her to renew her acquaintance with Margaret Bourke-White, one of the small handful of other female photographers whose careers were just getting started. In April 1929, when Berenice traveled to Cleveland to visit her mother, she also called on Margaret, who had recently completed a series of steel mill photographs that Berenice greatly admired. Thanks to these photographs, Bourke-White began receiving assignments from *Fortune* magazine. When the magazine's editors presented a portrait of Bourke-White to introduce her to their readers, they picked one that had been taken by Abbott.

Bourke-White went on to become one of the most celebrated figures in the newly emerging field of photojournalism, in which images are used to tell a news story. She was hired by *Life* as the magazine's first photographer in 1936, and her photograph of a dam in Montana appeared on the magazine's first cover. Still working for *Life,* she became the first woman permitted to photograph combat operations during World War II. She continued photographing for *Life* into the 1950s, covering the Korean War and operations of the Strategic Air Command.

Besides Bourke-White, Robert Capa, Alfred Eisenstaedt, and W. Eugene Smith are cited as some of photojournalism's leading practitioners. But Abbott never seemed to give much thought to that aspect of her profession. As the golden age of photojournalism was beginning to unfold, Abbott began photographing New York, and that became the ruling passion of her life.

6

"A Big Theme"

Berenice's first photographs of New York, taken in 1929, were made with her hand-held camera. She assembled about two hundred of these images in an ordinary photograph album with standard black pages. To Berenice these were no more than preliminary studies. "Just notes," she called them.

While she felt these photographs were satisfactory, she knew that she could do much better with a bigger camera, so she bought a Century-Universal view camera. It required the use of a tripod and took one photograph at a time on a large 8" x 10" film negative, from which prints of that size were made. Such cameras are often used today for commercial work, particularly architectural photographs. With its oversize negatives, the view camera produced prints that were finely detailed. Berenice's photographs were now deeper, richer, stronger.

The view camera also helped solve the problem of image distortion. When photographing a very tall building with a camera with an ordinary lens, Berenice often had to tilt the camera away from the structure in order to get the entire building into the frame. Doing this altered the image: The sides of the building would be slanted toward the top. The view camera had tilting adjustments at the front and back that overcame this failing.

Her big view camera enabled Abbott to take photographs rich in detail, as is apparent in her picture of a New York newsstand and its very readable magazine covers. (COMMERCE GRAPHICS LTD., INC.)

A drawback to the view camera was its size and weight. It was almost as big as a milk crate and very heavy, weighing almost forty pounds. Moving it, the tripod, cases, and other equipment from place to place was no easy matter. On Wednesdays, the day Berenice usually spent photographing the city, she not only wished for good weather, she also hoped to be able to find someone with a car she could borrow to tote her bulky camera and everything else from one location to another.

Just as Atget was often taunted by passersby, so it was with

Abbott. "I was shy about setting up my camera in New York," she said. "The first time I tried it I packed up and went home. But I knew I had to do it and I made myself come back."

One day Berenice lugged her equipment through Times Square and began setting up her camera before the eight-foot statue of soldier-priest Father Francis Patrick Duffy, a hero of World War I. The statue was tightly wrapped from head to toe in heavy blue cloth in preparation of its unveiling a few days later.

As Berenice adjusted the tripod and began focusing, several curious people stopped to watch. Soon the gathering became a sizable crowd. Then a police officer arrived. He scolded Berenice for creating a disturbance.

Berenice took one hurried photograph and then quickly packed up her equipment and left. "I wasn't smart about fighting back then," she recalled.

Men often made fun of Berenice. "Women did not wear slacks then; they wore skirts," Berenice recalled. "When I photographed New York, I put on ski pants. Truck drivers yelled at me, 'Lady, take that off.' It bothered me. But I found the way was to ignore them, as if they weren't there."

Almost from the beginning of her New York project, Berenice sought financial support for her work. Late in 1931 she approached the Museum of the City of New York for backing. While museum officials were impressed with her work, they told her there were no funds available for the project.

Later Berenice tried the New-York Historical Society. "Old New York is fast disappearing," Abbott wrote in her proposal "At almost any point on Manhattan Island the sweep of one's

When Abbott photographed the statue of Father Duffy in New York's Times Square, it was tightly wrapped in blue cloth in anticipation of the figure's unveiling ceremony. (COMMERCE GRAPHICS LTD., INC.)

vision can take in dramatic contrasts of the old and the new and the bold foreshadowing of the future. This dynamic quality should be caught and recorded immediately in a documentary interpretation of New York."

Her plea fell on deaf ears.

As one turndown for funding for the New York project followed another, Berenice sometimes felt discouraged. Nevertheless, she continued to photograph the city.

"Night View," a stunning photograph of New York after dark with office-building lights ablaze, one of Berenice's best-known images, is from this period. Filled with drama and energy, the photograph was taken from an upper floor of the Empire State Building and covers several blocks to the north and west, presenting the city as a glittering spectacle of light, its towering buildings jutting up from crisscrossed streets.

This photograph required an enormous amount of planning. There are only a few days a year when New York's office buildings are fully lighted against a night sky. These occur late in December, when the sun sets at approximately four-thirty P.M. Shortly after five P.M., when office workers end their day, the lights begin to be extinguished. Berenice realized that because she would be taking the photograph in conditions of extremely limited light, she would have to make a very long exposure, one that would last fifteen minutes.

These factors meant she would have no second chance. If she missed getting the picture, she would have to come back another afternoon or perhaps even the following year.

Her bird's-eye view of Trinity Church on Broadway in Lower Manhattan enabled Abbott to include the church's historic burial ground in the picture.
(COMMERCE GRAPHICS LTD., INC.)

Her advance planning paid off. Berenice got the photograph on her first try and was very happy with the results. She was surprised that the negative was as sharp as it was, because tall buildings often sway. Today "Night View" is arguably her most popular image.

Berenice's freelance magazine work provided her with most of her income during this period. But the work was erratic; she seldom had regular assignments to count on. Sometimes what she earned was barely enough for food, rent, and other essentials. When she was seriously broke, she would pay a visit to Romana Javitz, who headed the picture collection at the New York Public Library. Javitz loved Abbott's work and would purchase several original prints of her New York views for five or ten dollars each. The arrangement helped Berenice survive over the years. The purchases also served as a starting point for what would eventually become one of the largest collections of Abbott photographs.

In July 1933 an opportunity arose to make some money doing what she loved. Architectural historian Henry-Russell Hitchcock offered Berenice a job involving two projects. One was to photograph the Civil War–era architecture of a number of American cities. The other was to document the buildings of the architect Henry Hobson Richardson. Berenice spent six weeks on both projects during the summer of 1934, traveling with Hitchcock to Boston, Philadelphia, Baltimore, and Charleston, South Carolina.

Returning to New York, Berenice resumed the work that so absorbed her. By now her New York images were finally begin-

Of all of Abbott's New York photographs, "Night View," taken from the observation deck of the Empire State Building, is perhaps her most famous. (COMMERCE GRAPHICS LTD., INC.)

ning to attract attention. A selection of them was exhibited at Julien Levy's gallery and another at the Museum of the City of New York on the occasion of the opening of the museum's new building on Fifth Avenue in January 1932. There were other exhibitions in San Francisco; Hartford, Connecticut; and Springfield, Massachusetts.

In October 1934 the Museum of the City of New York presented a much larger exhibition of forty-six prints of Berenice's New York work, in what was her first one-person show in New York. The public loved it. Although the exhibit was scheduled to close in November, museum officials extended it to February 1935.

The show was a critical success, too. Newspapers and magazines were filled with glowing praise for Abbott's photographs. *The New Yorker* called for "miles and miles of such pictures."

Elizabeth McCausland, a critic for the *Springfield* (Massachusetts) *Republican,* lauded Abbott for choosing "a big theme" and for producing photographs that "succeeded in creating the spirit of the city."

When Abbott read McCausland's review, she was delighted. She wrote to McCausland, describing the article in the Springfield paper as "the first intelligent one on my work that has appeared in this country." Then she added, "I have and have had a fantastic passion for New York, photographically speaking."

McCausland later praised Abbott in a magazine article for the "sympathetic warmth and understanding" of her work and for her "deeply sincere effort to present the essential truth of her subject, whether the subject is the Chrysler Building or James Joyce."

In February 1935 that fantastic passion and her desire to pursue it resulted in Berenice's making yet another attempt for financial support. She dusted off her old proposal and applied for funding to the Federal Art Project (FAP), a relief agency for artists. The FAP had come into existence in 1935 as part of the Works Progress Administration (WPA), a massive government program created to provide work for the millions of Depression unemployed. It was one of several economic and social programs introduced by President Franklin D. Roosevelt and his administration. Those hired through the WPA and its agencies renovated schools and post offices, built roads and bridges, and constructed airports. But the WPA was unusual because it provided assistance to thousands whose jobs did not fit into any of the usual categories of relief. The Federal Art Project was one example.

In her proposal to the FAP, Berenice said that she wanted to be able "to capture the spirit of the metropolis, while remaining true to its essential fact, its hurrying tempo, its congested streets, the past jostling the future."

Weeks went by. Abbott heard nothing from the FAP.

Meanwhile, that spring Abbott met Elizabeth McCausland in person. Originally from Wichita, Kansas, and a couple of years younger than Abbott, McCausland had taken a job as a reporter for the *Springfield Republican* in 1923, after graduating from Smith College. Once she became the paper's art critic, her articles for the paper and a number of magazines earned her a place of prominence in the art world. McCausland was always very much a social activist, encouraging artists to consider the social and political aspects of their work as well as using it as a means of personal expression.

Abbott deeply admired McCausland for what she later called "her beautiful brain" and "extraordinary abilities, far beyond run of the mill." Abbott was willing to overlook the fact that McCausland was a friend of Stieglitz's and had a high opinion of his work. "We used to argue about that," Abbott said, "and maybe she saw things in Stieglitz I should [have] seen, and didn't."

Despite their occasional discord, Abbott and McCausland, whom Abbott called Butchy, formed a relationship that was to last for thirty years. McCausland was, said Abbott, "the best friend I ever had."

The summer of 1935 arrived, and Abbott had still not received a response from the FAP. She then decided to travel with McCausland and photograph rural America. The two drove from New York to St. Louis and then into the Deep South. Abbott took more than two hundred photographs of people suffering the agonies of the Depression in small-town America. It was not a pleasant undertaking for Abbott. She later remarked that she found it

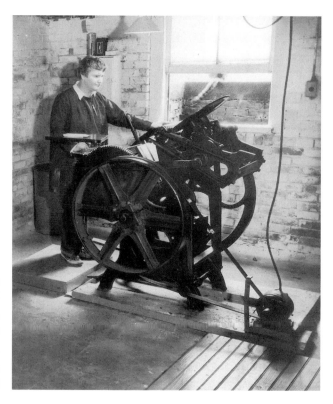

In addition to her talents as a writer, critic, and teacher, Elizabeth McCausland was skilled as a printer, and, when living in Springfield, Massachusetts, owned her own press, on which she turned out pamphlets and brochures.
(ARCHIVES OF AMERICAN ART, SMITHSONIAN INSTITUTION)

For thirty years, this former perfume factory in New York City's West Village was home to Abbott and McCausland. Out of place in a quiet residential neighborhood, it looks much the same today as it did in the 1930s.
(PHOTOGRAPH BY GEORGE SULLIVAN)

difficult "to stick a camera in the face of someone burdened with such poverty."

But McCausland remained enthusiastic about the project, and was further energized when some of Abbott's photographs from the trip were presented in a feature article in *The New York Times.* She and Berenice began talking about making an ambitious one-year tour of the country that would take them to each of the forty-eight states. The photographs that Berenice planned to take during the journey would be accompanied by text written by McCausland Together they would be used in a book, said McCausland, that would serve as "a portrait in words and photographs of the United States of America." But when Abbott and

McCausland tried to get funding for the project, their requests were turned down, and they didn't pursue the project further.

Later in the year Abbott and McCausland moved into separate apartments across the hallway from each other on the fourth floor of a six-story white brick building at 50 Commerce Street, on the western edge of Greenwich Village. The commercial-looking structure, once a perfume factory, seemed out of place in what was a quiet neighborhood of small townhouses on a winding and narrow street.

Berenice immediately set to work converting some of what had once been a storage area into a studio and darkroom. It was easy to make the room lightproof, because it had only one small window that looked out on a ventilation shaft. Because there was no natural light, Abbott had to use artificial light when making portraits, which didn't appeal to her. And since the space was practically airless, it reeked of chemicals once in operation.

Cooking odors from a restaurant on the first floor drifted up to the rooms Abbott and McCausland occupied. But Berenice didn't care. She now had enough space. And though it wasn't perfect, it was cheap.

For the next thirty years, 50 Commerce Street would be the home and workplace for Abbott and McCausland. Since they were both women of strong and sometimes opposing ideas and opinions, their relationship occasionally had its difficult moments. The two, however, encouraged and supported each other through the decades. Often they struggled as professionals, Abbott as a photographer, McCausland as a critic and freelance writer. But it was not a lonely struggle.

7

PICTURES OF A CHANGING CITY

In September 1935 Berenice got some exciting news. The Federal Art Project had finally approved her request for financial support while she photographed New York. Berenice would be getting from the FAP what she needed most, a regular paycheck. She was to be paid a monthly salary of $145, which would ease her financial worries and enable her to begin photographing New York on a full-time basis.

A steady income was only part of it. Berenice was also to be provided with a driver to help her transport her heavy, bulky camera and equipment through the city, a darkroom helper, and assistants to catalog her negatives and prints. Her staff was also to include two researchers to lend a hand in investigating the history of the sites that she photographed. The following year, 1936, the FAP even furnished Berenice with an automobile, a small Ford with a big trunk.

The Museum of the City of New York was to be the official sponsor of the project and agreed to provide Berenice with the photographic supplies she needed. The museum also agreed to purchase a set of prints once Berenice had completed her work.

At about the time that Berenice was getting established with the FAP, another government agency, the Farm Security Administration (FSA), was hiring photographers to record the plight of Americans trapped in the anguish of the Depression. Walker Evans, Ben Shahn, Dorothea Lange, Carl Mydans, and others began to document the hard times of coal miners, child laborers, sharecroppers, and Dust Bowl migrants. Their moving black-and-white studies helped to lift the nation to a new level of social awareness.

Berenice's situation was very different from that of the FSA photographers, who were given their assignments from the agency's Washington headquarters. Berenice was in charge of her project. She supervised a staff. She could photograph what she wanted whenever she wanted.

Berenice concentrated on Manhattan, with about half of her photographs devoted to the lower stretches of the borough. She paid little attention to the outer boroughs—the Bronx, Queens, Brooklyn, and Staten Island. In April 1936 she began calling the project "Changing New York."

Once she began, Berenice overlooked very little. She photographed mansions and tenements, hotels and apartment buildings, bars and restaurants, newsstands and antique shops, busy midtown intersections and quiet, narrow back streets. Occasionally she included people in her pictures, but her chief emphasis was on the physical structure of New York.

One day not long after she had begun working, an FAP supervisor looked with dismay at some of the pictures Berenice had taken on the Bowery, a neighborhood of cheap barrooms

For this picture of the intersection of Second and Third Avenue "el" lines, Abbott had to set up her camera on a tiny island in the middle of the street, with traffic streaming by on both sides. (COMMERCE GRAPHICS LTD., INC.)

and run-down hotels populated by alcoholics and homeless people. "Now, listen," the official said, "nice girls don't go to the Bowery."

Berenice was stunned. The idea that anyone could tell her where to go or not go appalled her. "I'm not a nice girl!" she shot back. "I'm a photographer!" The supervisor never bothered her again.

For many photographs Berenice needed permission to set up her camera. This was particularly true when she wanted to take a picture from one of the upper floors of a tall building. She often found building superintendents difficult to deal with. "They thought you wanted to commit suicide," she said. To grant their approval, they often had to be tipped or, as Berenice put it, "bribed."

Superintendents weren't the only problem with tall buildings. Berenice hated heights. It took enormous courage for her to lean out of the window on a skyscraper's upper floor, camera in hand, to take the photograph she wanted.

Manhattan's el systems—the city's elevated passenger railroads, now largely replaced by subways—were frequently her subject. In Lower Manhattan she photographed the heavy steelwork that formed the Second and Third Avenue lines. She captured the interior of an el station on the Ninth Avenue line. These elevated railroad lines endured in midtown and Lower Manhattan until the mid-1950s, when the last of them was torn down.

Berenice also photographed the Horn and Hardart Automats, popular self-service restaurants where food items were displayed in small glass-fronted compartments and purchased by dropping nickels into slots. By the early 1990s, all of the Automats had

To Abbott, New York's self-service restaurants known as Automats were uniquely American. In this Abbott photograph, a man selects and purchases a piece of pie from one of the compartments displaying food. (COMMERCE GRAPHICS LTD., INC.)

been torn down or converted to fast-food restaurants or other businesses. She also photographed the Old Post Office, a classic example of Victorian architecture at the southern tip of City Hall Park, which has since been demolished.

Berenice did not neglect New York's many ethnic neighborhoods, which came into existence following the great waves of immigrants, chiefly from southern and eastern Europe, who flooded into the city in the final decades of the nineteenth cen-

tury. Often she photographed storefronts that represented these different cultures. Her pictures included a kosher butcher on the Lower East Side, a Lebanese restaurant on the Lower West Side, and an Italian bakery in Greenwich Village.

Abbott's popular Blossom Restaurant photograph was taken in the fall of 1935. The restaurant occupied the ground floor of the Boston Hotel at 103 Bowery. The hotel was what was known as a flophouse, one of many in the area where rooms could be rented cheaply. The tiny rooms, each furnished with a cot and not much else, cost thirty cents a night. "The man [in the photo] came out when he saw me setting up the camera," Abbott told Hank O'Neal, her biographer. "He stood there not knowing what to do, and since I was ready I made the photograph with him in the doorway. He makes it much better."

In Lower Manhattan in the summer of 1936, Abbott photographed an "urban canyon" by standing in Exchange Place, a couple of blocks south of Wall Street, facing Broadway, and pointing her camera upward. The Adams Building, at the center of the photograph, still stands. Modern skyscrapers have replaced the other buildings in the photo.

Abbott had produced a very different image when she had photographed the site earlier, in 1932. From the tenth floor of the Adams Building itself, Abbott aimed her camera straight down Exchange Place, which made the steep-sided canyon walls much more apparent. "I had devised a very low tripod that I used for shooting out windows," Abbott recalled. "It had adjustable legs that could be used on windowsills. I used it here."

Abbott's photographs of New York storefronts—such as this picture of a kosher chicken market on the city's Lower East Side—were evidence of the city's ethnic diversity. (COMMERCE GRAPHICS LTD., INC.)

Abbott photographed the Flatiron Building, a well-known Manhattan landmark, several times. One of New York's first skyscrapers, the twenty-story building dates to 1902 and occupies a wedge-shaped piece of land where Broadway cuts across Twenty-third Street. The building that fills the triangle resembles an old-fashioned flatiron, used to press clothing.

Abbott's first photograph of the building was taken from the tenth floor of a building just to the north. It shows the Flatiron

Abbott's photograph of the Blossom Restaurant. (COMMERCE GRAPHICS LTD., INC.)

Canyon-like Exchange Place, a very narrow street framed by skyscrapers in New York's financial district, attracted Abbott and her camera on several occasions. For this view, she mounted her camera on the windowsill of a close-by skyscraper and took the picture through the window. (COMMERCE GRAPHICS LTD., INC.)

When the towering office buildings that form Rockefeller Center were being built in the 1930s, Abbott often visited the site to record the progress of construction. (COMMERCE GRAPHICS LTD., INC.)

Building in relation to the busy streets that border it, as well as several neighboring buildings.

Abbott preferred a later photograph, taken in 1938. Standing in traffic, she got much closer to the building and pointed her camera upward, clipping the upper floors from the base. A much stronger image resulted.

When Abbott photographed the triangular-shaped Flatiron Building, one of New York City's first skyscrapers, in 1938, she got the best results by setting up her camera at ground level. (COMMERCE GRAPHICS LTD., INC.)

Berenice took several photographs of the Empire State Building, which began going up in 1930. However, she was much more interested in Rockefeller Center. Early in the 1930s she began photographing its construction site, taking extraordinary views as workers cut far into the bedrock. She returned to the site many times over the next few years, photographing the rising pile of structural steel from different angles and heights. She photographed one of the completed skyscrapers in the Rockefeller Center complex in 1937.

During the years she photographed New York, Abbott often suffered from what she called "technological frustration." She constantly struggled with the cameras, film, and lenses of the time. They often wouldn't do what she wanted them to do.

Cameras failed her, she felt, when she was seeking to achieve depth of field (also called depth of focus). Depth of field is the zone in which objects on the film are in sharp focus. If the nearest in-focus object is ten feet from the camera and the farthest object in sharp focus is twenty feet away, then the image on the film has a depth of field of ten feet.

The chief factor affecting depth of field in a photograph is the size of the lens opening. The smaller the lens opening, the greater the depth of field.

Berenice's problem in trying to achieve depth of field came in conditions of poor light, when she was attempting to freeze the action of the moment. Suppose, she said, "[y]ou want to take a subway rush at 5 o'clock at 150th of a second—which you need to stop motion. What can you do? You have to open your lens up . . .

New York City lost one of its architectural treasures when the original Pennsylvania Station, pictured here in a dramatic interior shot by Abbott, was demolished in 1963. (COMMERCE GRAPHICS LTD., INC.)

and sacrifice detail in the background. The only thing sharp will be your first three rows."

"Cameras are primitive today," she noted in 1938. "There is no excuse for their primitiveness. There is not one good camera. There are lots of things I could have taken in the last five years," she added, "if I only had had better cameras."

As Berenice continued to work on "Changing New York," she began to attract enthusiastic praise. Newspapers started writing about her on a regular basis. Magazines like *Popular Photography* and *U.S. Camera* sought her photographs and sent writers to interview her. *Life* magazine devoted several pages to the project.

More and more frequently, Berenice's photographs were being exhibited in galleries and museums. Late in 1937 the Museum of the City of New York held an exhibition of 111 of Abbott's "Changing New York" photographs. It was more than twice the size of the Abbott show presented by the museum in 1934. Nine New York newspapers ran feature articles about the exhibition, and several of them included profiles of Abbott. Also in 1937 Yale University held an Abbott exhibition.

The writer and photographer Carl Van Vechten, a fixture on the New York art scene, wrote to Berenice to say: "I went to see your New York pictures yesterday and you wouldn't need to be told they were all completely magnificent. They have clarity and sympathy. Technically they are flawless. I must say I find you pretty much the master (or mistress) of all living photographers."

The Abbott show at the Museum of the City of New York was so popular that it was extended for six weeks. Its great success

It was rush hour, and the corner of Fifth Avenue and 42nd Street was jammed with office workers, shoppers, and tourists when Abbott leaned out of the window of a tall office building to make this photograph. (COMMERCE GRAPHICS LTD., INC.)

helped to induce E. P. Dutton and Company of New York to publish a book in 1939 called *Changing New York* that included close to one hundred of Berenice's photographs. Elizabeth Mc-Causland wrote the captions.

When *Changing New York* was first published, Berenice was again nudged into the limelight. In reviewing the book, Beaumont Newhall, a notable figure in American photography as an author, teacher, and scholar, declared that Berenice's work "represents the best in documentary photography today."

As praise for Berenice's work grew louder, her relationship with the FAP was heading downhill. Government programs that provided aid to artists, who were regarded by some members of Congress as loafers or worse, were subject to constant criticism. By the late 1930s conservatives in Congress became outright hostile toward the FAP and other such agencies. They began stripping them of their power and slashing their budgets. The FAP was one of the agencies they targeted. Berenice's salary was reduced and her staff dissolved. She left the FAP in 1939.

Before she ended her connection with "Changing New York," Berenice made a set of 305 signed and mounted prints for the Museum of the City of New York from hundreds of photographs she had taken. These, along with 700 of her negatives, as well as the files of the project's researchers, are part of the museum's collection today.

Berenice's New York photographs are an American treasure. Straightforward, strong, and precise, they form one of the truly

When it comes to New York's bridges, most photographers prefer the Brooklyn Bridge as a subject. Abbott, however, liked the Manhattan Bridge, the Brooklyn Bridge's neighbor just to the north. Looking straight up, she focused her camera on the decorative design created by the bridge's rivets, railings, and cables.

(COMMERCE GRAPHICS LTD., INC.)

exceptional bodies of work in the history of modern photography. Berenice approached the project with great enthusiasm, with the feeling that she was photographing something almost unseen or unknown. Many of her photographs express this exuberance.

Taken as a whole, Berenice's New York photographs are unique in another sense. Although she photographed New York during the worst years of the Depression, she rarely used her camera to document its effects in human terms. There are no photographs of homeless persons asleep in doorways, none of destitute men selling apples on street corners, and none of the long lines of people waiting for food handouts.

At the time Berenice was photographing New York, Walker Evans, Ben Shahn, and others of the FSA photographers were documenting the plight of dirt-poor farmers and migrants during the Depression. Lewis Hine, decades earlier, had traveled widely to photograph young children working in mines, factories, and sweatshops.

But Berenice preferred to let Hine, Evans, and others use photography as social commentary, producing images that could evoke sorrow or despair. Bridges, tall buildings, and city streets were her choice. She had no wish to thrust herself into the lives of others, just as she would not permit her own life to be intruded upon.

Berenice was absorbed in photographing New York for almost a full decade. When the project drew to an end, she realized that she had fulfilled her fantastic passion. It was time to move on, to find another worthy subject. And she had a different kind of subject in mind. Once begun, it would turn out to be even more challenging than documenting New York. In time, the project would help to create a whole new field of photography.

8

TEACHER, AUTHOR, INVENTOR

While the "Changing New York" project was the most important feature in Berenice's life for the decade beginning in 1929, it wasn't her only interest. She involved herself in a variety of other activities during that time. She wrote articles and arranged exhibitions of her photographs, and occasionally she busied herself with portrait photography.

In the spring of 1934 a portrait assignment helped to open yet another career path for her. She had been asked to photograph the head of the New School for Social Research at the school's headquarters in New York. As the session was nearing its end, the official told Berenice that the school was planning on introducing a course in photography in the fall and asked if she would be interested in teaching it.

The offer took Berenice by surprise. She hardly knew what to say.

Founded in 1919, the New School for Social Research (The New School) was making a pioneering effort to provide university-quality education for adult students. The founders were some of the most distinguished educators of the day. They included historian Charles Beard, philosopher John Dewey, economist John Maynard Keynes, and editor and writer W. E. B. DuBois.

The New School looks much as it did during the more than two decades Abbott taught there, from the mid-1930s to the late 1950s.
(PHOTOGRAPH BY GEORGE SULLIVAN)

The school had recently moved into its new home, a striking example of modernist architecture on West Twelfth Street in Greenwich Village. While already notable for exploring social issues, the New School was beginning to offer classes in the arts. The school hired Martha Graham, a world-renowned teacher of dance who had trained and inspired countless front-rank dancers and choreographers, and Aaron Copland, arguably the foremost American composer.

Berenice felt flattered that she would be asked to join such a distinguished teaching staff. But the offer also made her uneasy. Because of her shyness, the very idea of teaching filled her with anxiety. Of course she had taught American-style dancing in Paris years before. But that was different. She was involved with her students as individuals. Now she would be confronted by a large group of men and women in a classroom setting. "I'd probably faint and have to be carried out," she thought.

Berenice's shyness wasn't her only problem. Years before, when she had worked with Man Ray in his Paris studio, they had often used French in speaking to each other about photographic technology. A print was an *épreuve*. A developing tray was a *cuvette*. Ever since, Berenice had continued to think of the words and terms connected with photography in the French language. She realized that if she were to teach, she would always be translating such terms back into English. It could be confusing.

But the more she thought about the offer, the more she felt she ought to accept it. Of course, it would be difficult for her. But perhaps the course would help her to tame the shyness that still plagued her. That would make it worthwhile.

Abbott began teaching at the New School in the fall of 1935. She once referred to the experience as "the most terrifying thing I ever did." It took her almost two years before she began to feel comfortable in front of a class.

Abbott taught her Workshop in Photography class one evening a week. It was a practical course, meant to instruct students in the basics of lenses, cameras, lighting, printing, and the like.

In this and other courses she would later teach, Berenice frowned upon the use of popular point-and-shoot cameras. She instead encouraged her students to use a twin-lens reflex camera.

Held at waist level, the twin-lens reflex camera was designed in such a way that an image of the picture being taken is reflected from a mirror onto a square of glass at the camera's top. (The glass, called ground glass, is not transparent, having had its pol-

Abbott wanted each of her New School students to use a twin-lens reflex camera like this one. The upper lens reflected the image onto a glass viewing screen at the top of the camera. (KOMAMORA CORPORATION)

ished surface removed by fine grinding.) Berenice wanted her students to see things as they are, whether they were photographing a sunset, a city street, or children at play. The viewing system of the twin-lens reflex camera enables one to do that.

By the fall of 1936 Berenice was teaching two workshop courses a week, one for beginners, the second for advanced students. She later taught advanced photography techniques by means of weekly field trips, where students, according to the New School catalog, learned "such tasks as a professional photographer meets in real-life assignments."

"There were a few talented students but not too many," Berenice said. "The best you can do in a course like that is help students to find themselves . . . to have the courage to be themselves. I never showed them any of my photographs. I didn't want to influence them. I wanted them to find their own way."

Some of Berenice's students went on to become respected professional photographers. A number had photographs published by *Life* magazine.

Berenice continued at the New School until 1958. But she did more than merely teach. Through the years she encouraged other noted photographers to join the teaching staff, which helped to make the New School one of the nation's leading institutions in photography education, a reputation it has maintained to this day.

Teaching photography courses at the New School produced another and unforeseen benefit. Berenice was able to use her class notes and the personal knowledge she had gained in teaching to write a how-to book on photography. It covered topics ranging from buying a camera to taking pictures to printing and developing.

The first publisher Berenice approached about the book liked the idea. *A Guide to Better Photography* was published in 1941 and well received.

In a chapter titled "A Point of View" Berenice expressed her disapproval of pictorialists, the photographers who used the "artistic" techniques she so despised, often softening the focus or altering their prints in the darkroom. To these photographers, what was in front of the camera was of secondary importance.

Berenice accused pictorialists of "devious manipulation." With their use of ink, paint, charcoal, or the like, they created "prettiness." She quoted the American essayist and poet Ralph Waldo Emerson, who once wrote, "Avoid prettiness, the word looks much like pettiness, and there is but little difference between them." Said Berenice: "Photography is to communicate the realities of life, the facts which are to be seen everywhere about us."

Besides teaching at the New School and writing, Berenice occupied her time by attempting to turn some of the many ideas for new kinds of photographic equipment that buzzed about in her active mind. Simply stated, she became an inventor. She formed a small company called the House of Photography to finance and promote the sale of what she invented.

Berenice was responsible for creating some remarkable tools. Several earned her government patents. None, however, produced very much money. Most of the income the House of Photography managed to generate was paid out to lawyers and those who created the prototypes, based on Berenice's designs, from which the inventions could be produced.

One of Berenice's creations was a Band-Aid–size strip of rubbery material that was treated with adhesive on both sides, used for hanging pictures. This did away with the necessity of ham-

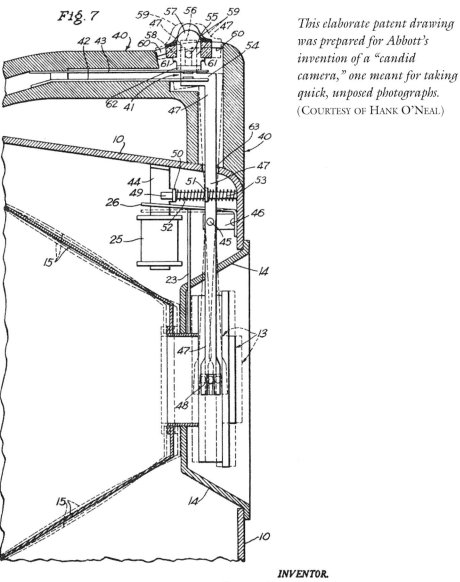

F1g. 7

This elaborate patent drawing was prepared for Abbott's invention of a "candid camera," one meant for taking quick, unposed photographs.
(COURTESY OF HANK O'NEAL)

INVENTOR.
Berenice Abbott

mering a hole in the wall. Today, this invention takes the form of double-sided adhesive tape that is commonly used to stick a picture to a wall or almost any other surface.

Another clever invention of hers was a floor-to-ceiling hollow metal pole. Springs at each end held the pole firmly in position, regardless of how high the ceiling was. Studio lights could then be attached to the pole at any level. Berenice called the invention a cat pole.

Berenice also created a jacket for photographers that was fitted with twenty or so pockets for carrying small items—extra rolls of film, filters, lens caps, a notebook, pencils, anything. Modern-day versions of the jacket and cat pole are now widely used by photographers.

One of Berenice's inventions was meant mostly for fun. Called the Abbott Distorter, it could be used to render a photograph into an absurd shape during the printing stage. The results looked as if the photograph had been taken in a funhouse mirror. "Amaze all by the impossibility of your shots," said Abbott's flyer promoting the device.

What Abbott had learned about chemistry, electronics, and physical principles through her experience developing new products and processes helped to steer her toward her next "worthy project." After she had completed Changing New York in 1939 and was seeking a new challenge, she made a decision to try her hand at photographing science. "We live in a world made by science," she noted. "But we . . . do not understand or appreciate the knowledge which thus controls daily life." What was needed, Berenice felt, was a friendly interpreter, a voice, to help the average person to understand and appreciate scientific principles. Photography could play that role, with Berenice herself wielding the camera. This, she believed, would be a logical evolution of her as a photographer.

She realized she would be taking on an enormous project. Her role, as she expressed it, would be "like that of a flea attacking a giant."

The Abbott distorter produced this twisted image of Abbott's self-portrait that appears on page 63. (THE MUSEUM OF MODERN ART)

Indeed, the task was probably more ambitious than Berenice herself realized. "Changing New York" was a project that absorbed her for ten years. Documenting scientific principles would prove to be an even more difficult undertaking, one that would involve her from 1939 into the 1960s.

Since she had little knowledge or training in science, Berenice set out to educate herself. She bought and studied books on physics and electricity. She took courses in chemistry at New York University.

The knowledge she acquired, however, could not help her solve the many technical problems she faced. Photographic equipment of the time was simple and crude in comparison to what is available today. Film was "slow," lacking in sensitivity, for the photographs she wanted to take. Long exposures were necessary as a result. Lighting was never strong enough. Cameras were unsuitable except for the most routine photographs.

Berenice worked hard to solve these problems. "For two years I have been working on a secret lighting process," she said in an interview in *Popular Photography* in 1942. "My new process is in the stage of evaluation before it can be hatched in full bloom."

The secret lighting process involved a huge camera that she built herself. She called it her Supersight camera. Five feet tall and three feet wide, the camera was big enough to hold a standing child. Its size wasn't the only thing unusual about her creation. The object to be photographed was to be placed *inside* the camera. The image was projected through a lens onto sensitized paper, producing a picture that was 16" x 20" in size.

With the Supersight camera, Berenice generated photographs

The soap bubbles in this photograph are tiny, but Abbott made them look big by fitting her camera with a macro lens. She lighted the arrangement from beneath the glass tray holding the suds. (COMMERCE GRAPHICS LTD., INC.)

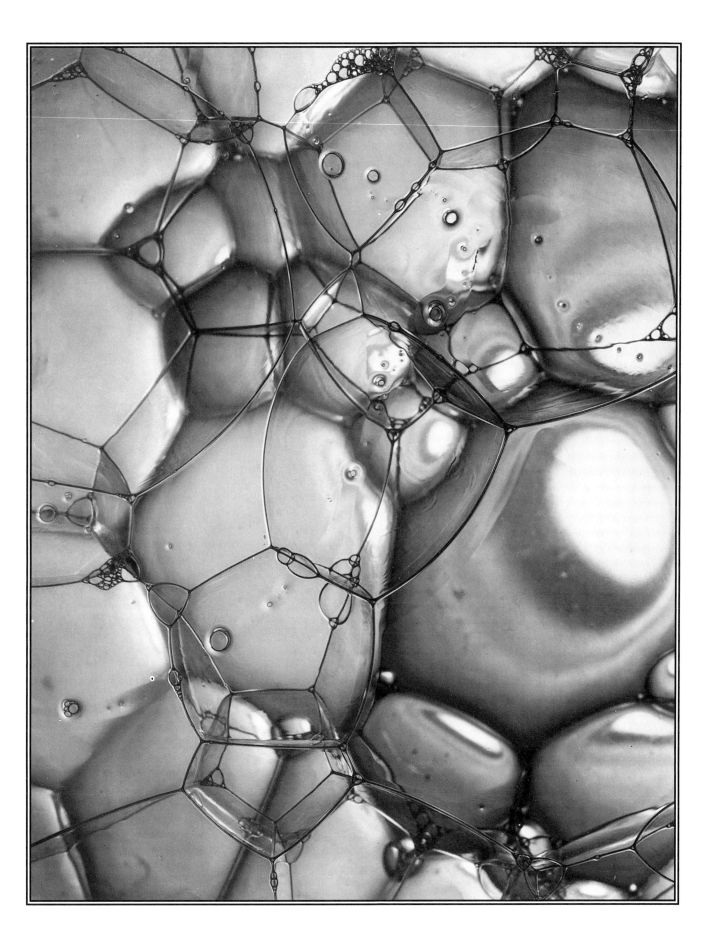

that were poster size of leaves, insects, blades of grass, penicillin mold, and the feather patterns in a bird's wing. They had enormous clarity and a great range of tones. Some of the objects she photographed seemed as if they could be perceived by touch.

Abbott's experimentation helped her land a job with *Science Illustrated* in 1944. It was her responsibility to provide dramatic photographs to illustrate articles in the magazine. Sometimes she used existing photographs; other times she created new images.

Unfortunately, the job did not last long. After a year new owners took over and changed the magazine's content. Berenice resigned. The issue of April 1945 was the last in which Berenice's name appeared as photographic editor.

One of the photographs that Berenice produced for *Science Illustrated* is perhaps her best-known science image. It depicts a glass tray of soap bubbles, showing in striking detail the composition of each. Berenice spent three days creating the photograph.

In the years that followed her brief stay at *Science Illustrated*, Berenice continued to interest herself in science photography. She truly believed that a need existed for clear, simple, straightforward images that would illustrate scientific principles. Getting the scientific community to realize this was the problem.

9

FOCUSING ON SCIENCE

Berenice's confidence got a boost in the late 1940s when Doubleday & Company, a leading New York publisher, offered to bring out a book of her science photographs, many of which she had taken with her Supersight camera. There was a hitch, however. Doubleday first wanted the Museum of Modern Art in New York to agree to exhibit the images as examples of experimental photography.

But when Edward Steichen, the newly appointed director of photography at the Modern, examined the photographs, he declared them to be trivial, of no importance. There would be no exhibition. There would be no book.

Few art museums were interested in photography at the time. But when Steichen had taken over as director of photography at the Modern in 1947, he broke new ground by displaying the work of dozens of photographers. From the time he joined the museum until his departure in 1962, Steichen presented forty-four photography exhibits. In so doing, he excited the interest of professional photographers and amateurs—anyone, in fact, with a serious interest in the craft.

For Abbott, however, Steichen, whom some regard as one of

history's greatest photographers, was a never-ending source of frustration. His view of photography was wholly different from hers. Steichen's early work as a photographer was often pictorial in style. Sometimes he would deliberately set his lens out of focus. Or he might sprinkle drops of water on the lens before taking a photograph to get an unusual effect. Abbott despised such tinkering.

The mere mention of Steichen's name brought a scowl to Abbott's face. "Steichen is an example of a small person who got into a position of power and used it for his own ends," she said. "He ran roughshod over me."

Time after time, Steichen turned his back on Abbott. What made this pill even more bitter to swallow was the fact that Steichen was among the first to advance the cause of women photographers at a time when only a handful were recognized as professionals. He believed that women were especially gifted when it came to photography, that they were aided by an intuitive sense. "Intuition is simply keen perception and evaluation," Steichen said. "[Women] know how to value their perception, which is something a man is very poor at as a rule."

Steichen exhibited the work of a number of women at the Modern: Margaret Bourke-White; Dorothea Lange, the most prominent of the FSA photographers; Lisette Model, well known for her political and cultural photographs; Esther Bubley, a photojournalist and documentary photographer; Helen Levitt, who concentrated on the social life of New York; and Imogen Cunningham, who excelled in portrait photography and, like Berenice, was a pioneer of modernism. He ignored Abbott.

Berenice shrugged off the snub. She never liked being singled out as a "woman photographer." She thought of herself as a photographer. Period.

By now Berenice had been a photographic artist for almost thirty years. She had been one of the two most successful portrait photographers in Paris during the late 1920s, if not *the* most successful. Her "Changing New York" project was what one critic called "one of the single greatest visual chronicles of a major American city." She was the author of several highly acclaimed books, including *A Guide to Better Photography* and *Greenwich*

Village, Today and Yesterday, published in 1949, a book that offered views of the twisting streets, landmark buildings, small shops and markets to be found in the section of the city that she knew so well. She had rescued the photographs and negatives of Eugène Atget, the master French photographer. Yet Edward Steichen scarcely seemed to recognize her existence.

Berenice made no effort to close the breach. If anything, she worsened the situation by continuing to express her opinions openly, not seeming to care about the consequences.

Early in October 1951 she was invited to speak at an important photography conference at the Aspen Institute of Humanistic Studies in Colorado. Photography historians, critics, and some of the best-known photographers of the time attended the ten-day event. Those taking part wanted to discuss the status of their profession and their role in the world in which they lived and worked.

Berenice looked forward to the conference. It was a chance for her to renew friendships. But she also saw it as another opportunity to express her long-held beliefs about photography.

When it came her turn to speak, Berenice was filled with anxiety. "My knees were sort of quaking," she later recalled. "I thought God might descend from the skies and strike me dead." But she did not hold back. "The greatest influence obscuring the field has been pictorialism," she began. "Pictorialism means chiefly the making of pleasant pretty pictures in the spirit of certain minor painters.

"Photography can never grow up and stand on its own two feet if it imitates some other medium," she said. "It has to walk alone."

In her fifties, Abbott worked hard but often faced difficult times. (ART INSTITUTE OF CHICAGO/PHOTOGRAPH BY PETER POLLACK)

She singled out Steichen, Stieglitz, and Paul Strand, Stieglitz's protégé, for special criticism. Said Abbott: "They were what I can only call for want of a better word, the advanced, or super-pictorialist school. The tendency here was to be very precious, very exclusive, very jealous of authority, excluding all others who would enter the sanctified portals of art."

These were curious comments for Abbott to make. Stieglitz and Steichen had turned from pictorialism years before. In the photography world, pictorialism was no longer an issue.

Not only were her remarks hard to explain, they were self-destructive. After her talk at Aspen, Abbott had some difficult days. There were few assignments from magazines. There was very little portrait work. For income she continued to rely chiefly on the New School for Social Research. She was now teaching as many as three courses each semester. As a professional photographer, she was, as one colleague put it, "out of the swim."

Furthermore, in her fifties now, Berenice believed that she was often being treated unfairly because of her age. "If you went up to see some editor," she recalled, "you met some young person who never heard of you in their life. They would treat you almost like a student, with, 'Well, leave your name and address.' That sort of thing. This was too much. I couldn't take it."

Out of her frustration, Berenice Abbott turned once again to the publishing field. She hit upon an idea of reprinting many of the portraits that she had made in France some thirty years before and presenting them in a book to be titled *Faces of the Twentieth Century*. But she was unable to interest any publishers in the project.

Another of Abbott's ideas was much more ambitious, almost on a par with "Changing New York". She made up her mind to photograph the cities and small towns along U.S. Route 1, which stretched along the Atlantic seaboard from Fort Kent, Maine, to Key West, Florida, a distance of 1,919 miles.

A young man named Damon Gadd, who ran a ski lodge in Vermont and was interested in photography, agreed to serve as

The Melbourne Hotel in Melbourne, Florida, was one of Abbott's subjects on her Maine-to-Florida trip along U.S. Route 1. (COMMERCE GRAPHICS LTD., INC.)

her driver. Abbott looked upon the project as an enormous challenge. Her ambition was to document the special character and diversity of the country through which she traveled, just as her New York photographs had revealed the city's uniqueness. Unfortunately, when she showed examples of her work to editors and publishers, they expressed little interest in them.

In 1955, when Berenice was still involved with her Route 1 photographs, she suffered another and perhaps even more serious rebuff at the hands of Edward Steichen when he presented an exhibition called "The Family of Man" at the Museum of Modern Art. It was the single most famous exhibition of photographs ever held. It earned Steichen legendary status.

With 503 photos representing sixty-eight countries, the exhibition was meant to illustrate man's journey through life. It received overwhelming public response. Nearly nine million people in thirty-seven countries eventually saw it.

Its importance in the world of photography cannot be overestimated. In reviewing the exhibition, the *New York Herald-Tribune* noted: "It can truly be said that with this show photography has come of age as a medium of expression and an art form."

The Family of Man represented the work of 257 photographers, 163 of them American. Berenice Abbott was not one of them.

Berenice faced a grim future. Her inventions had produced no income to speak of. One publisher after another had rejected her book proposals. There was no commercial work for her. She was beginning to feel depressed.

Then one day in 1957, history changed, and Berenice's life changed with it. On October 4 the Soviet Union, a group of fifteen countries in eastern Europe and Asia that included Russia, successfully launched Sputnik, the world's first artificial satellite. About the size of a basketball, and weighing 183 pounds, Sputnik kicked off a fierce race between the United States and the Soviet Union for supremacy in space.

To more than a few observers, the Soviet success indicated that the United States had fallen behind in the teaching of science. Various agencies of the federal government moved immediately to address the shortcoming.

Abbott quickly realized that she had a role to play in all that was happening. Her years of work in science photography could now have real value, she thought.

At the Massachusetts Institute of Technology (MIT) in Cambridge, the Physical Sciences Study Committee (PSSC) began examining science education at schools in the United States. New courses were being planned. New textbooks were to be written.

The PSSC needed a photographer who could help communicate the principles of modern science to those who knew little about the subject. By February 1958 Abbott had made her way to the PSSC in Cambridge. There she met with Dr. E. P. Little of MIT. When she showed some of her science photographs to Dr. Little, he looked at them and nodded. "This is just what we want," he said. "When can you start?"

Berenice's career was about to be reenergized. Her meeting with Dr. Little compares to the time thirty-five years earlier when Man Ray offered her a job as his assistant, a job that put her on the path to achievement and success. Abbot's encounter with Dr. Little would do much the same.

Berenice began work for the PSSC right away. She continued teaching at the New School until the spring semester ended, then gave up her teaching post and rented an apartment in Cambridge so that she could devote herself fully to the PSSC project.

Her new job, which involved expressing scientific truths in visual terms, was a stern test of her talents. Each physical principle that she sought to picture presented a different array of problems, and there were no examples from the past that could be followed. She would be breaking new ground. Special photo-

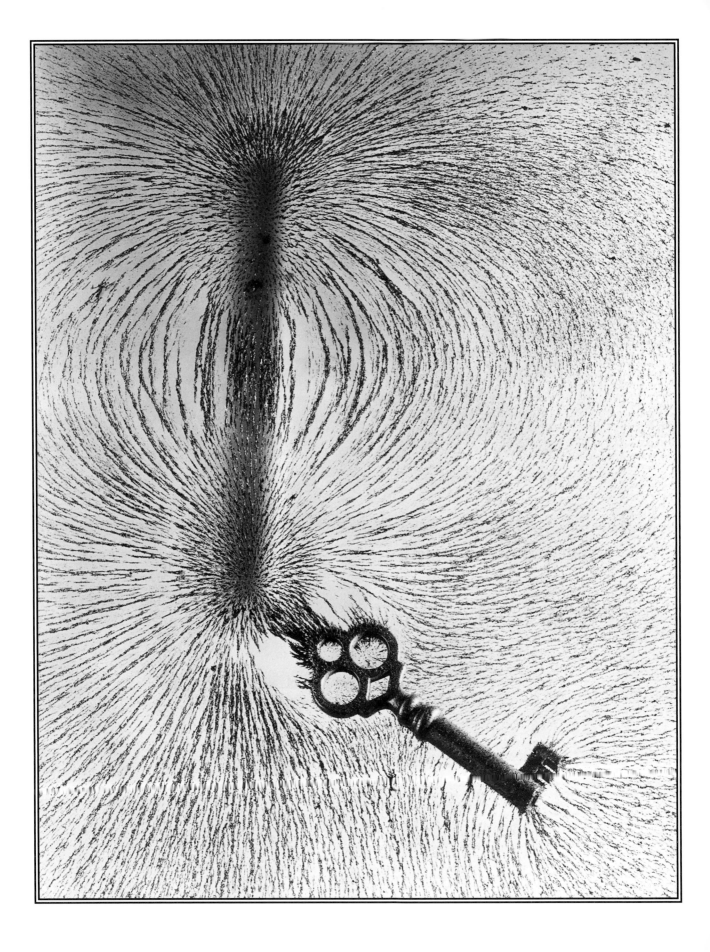

graphic equipment would have to be designed. Unique lighting systems would have to be created. Sometimes complete sets would have to be built, like those used in shooting a movie or staging a play.

One assignment was to illustrate the magnetic field around a bar magnet. Berenice did this with tiny particles that resulted from filing steel. She first sprinkled the filings onto a thin sheet of white cardboard. Since it was difficult to space the filings evenly, she ended up blowing them onto the cardboard through a straw.

When the magnet was held underneath the cardboard, the filings arranged themselves in a distinctive pattern. Berenice's photograph revealed the makeup of the magnetic field. In another shot, a key was added to the filings to show how its presence changed the magnetic pattern.

When asked to show a bouncing ball in motion, Berenice had a ball painted white and then lit with photoflood lamps against a black background. An opaque black disc with a slit cut in it was placed in front of the camera, as close as possible to the lens. Just before the ball was put into the air, the disc was made to spin rapidly. The camera took a photograph every time the slot passed in front of the lens. Photographing the ball at fixed intervals made it appear as if it had been stopped in midair.

Three bounces were recorded in each sequence. The photograph shows how the maximum height of the ball decreased with each bounce as the ball lost energy. The photograph also revealed how the ball's velocity varied within each bounce. The velocity slowed as the ball reached its maximum height, then speeded up as the ball fell.

Berenice's famous photograph of a spinning wrench used a

The pattern created by iron filings around a bar magnet is captured in this photograph. (COMMERCE GRAPHICS LTD., INC.)

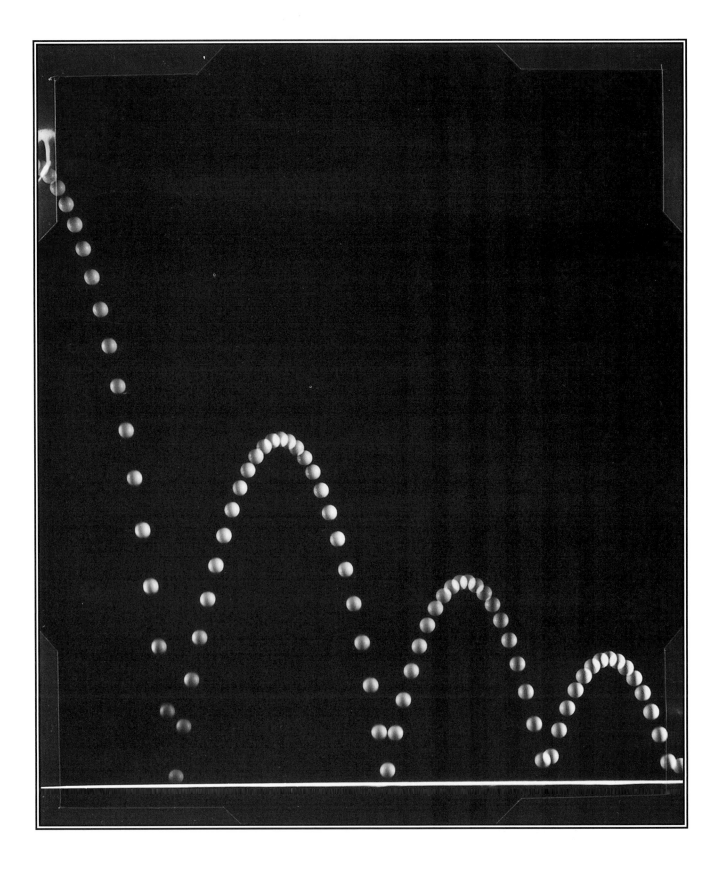

strobe—an electronic flash that produced rapid, brilliant bursts of light. The wrench was painted white, and a black X was placed at its center of gravity. Berenice mounted a stepladder with her camera and pointed the lens downward, focusing on the wrench. When an assistant released the wrench, it traveled from left to right, making one full spin. Berenice's striking sequence photograph showed that as the wrench spun in what appeared to be an erratic pattern, its center of gravity—the X—traveled in a perfectly straight line.

Once Berenice started producing photographs for the PSSC, they began appearing in magazines and newspapers. They were also featured in several books for young readers. The collection of photographs was later made available to the Smithsonian Institution and circulated to schools and museums throughout the United States.

Berenice's association with the PSSC ended on a dismal note in 1960. One day she was told that her photographs were no longer needed and her job was to be abolished. Berenice accepted the decision, offered her resignation, gave up her Cambridge apartment, and returned to New York and her Commerce Street home. She later learned that the job had not really been eliminated but had been given to someone else. "They got me out and hired my assistant instead, because he was younger and cheaper," said Berenice. "I was never so heartbroken in my life."

To illustrate the reduction of energy in a moving object, Abbott photographed a golf ball that had been rolled from a horizontal surface about six feet above a stretch of marble floor. (NEW YORK PUBLIC LIBRARY)

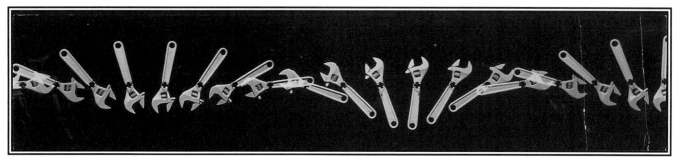

Days of preparation and practice were required before Abbott was able to make this notable spinning-wrench photograph. (New York Public Library)

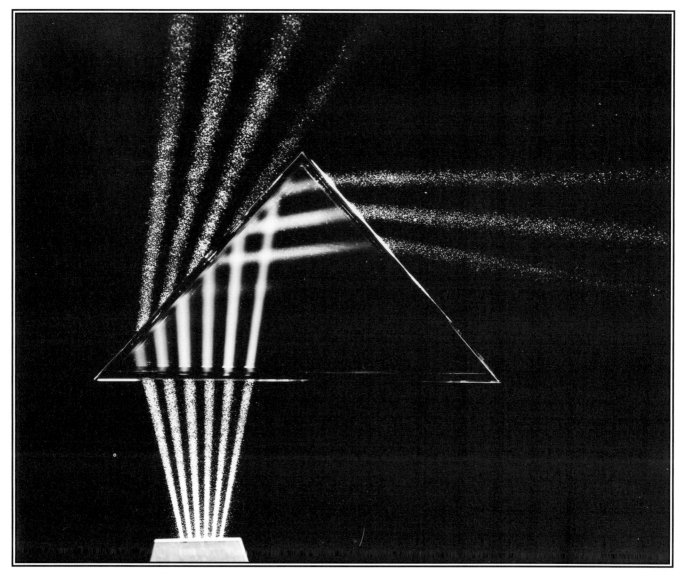

For this experiment showing the multiple paths light rays take through a prism, Abbott placed the light source beneath the prism, then directed the rays upward. (Commerce Graphics Ltd., Inc.)

In the years that followed, Berenice's science photographs continued to earn her recognition and renown. She had used her camera and film to produce images that could never be seen by the naked human eye. She was not merely *taking* photographs; she was *making* photographs.

Hank O'Neal declared: "[The science photographs] not only present the laws of physics as exciting, well-conceived, exquisitely printed photographs, but they also reveal an artist confidently at work, focusing her camera and her talent on a subject for which she had great awe." O'Neal and others felt that her science photographs might well be viewed in future years as Abbott's most outstanding contribution to photography.

10

An Awakening Interest

Berenice's project of photographing the cities and towns along Route 1 from Maine to Florida never resulted in the book she planned. And the burdensome travel expenses left her with a shriveled bank account. But some good came out of the undertaking. The project opened her eyes to the glories of the state of Maine. "I liked it better than any state on the entire Atlantic seaboard," she said.

Berenice confessed to friends that she was "crazy about Maine" and was even thinking about moving there. Then she learned of an unusual house available in the town of Blanchard, a tiny community of fewer than a hundred people in the central part of the state. A former stagecoach inn, the 150-year-old house could be purchased for only four hundred dollars. That made it affordable, even for Berenice.

On a visit to Blanchard in 1955, Berenice was thrilled by the beauty of the area, a boundless land of trees and lakes and rocks as big as Cadillacs. New York was more than a full day's drive away, but it seemed even more distant than that. It was quiet in Blanchard. Just breathing the crisp, clean air put Berenice in high spirits.

The house was huge, but it had been neglected for years and

needed a great deal of fixing up to make it livable. Even though the price had risen to eight hundred dollars, Berenice gave the owner a ten-dollar deposit and asked for a few weeks to make up her mind.

In the days after, Berenice kept thinking she could never find a house that cheap again. She wrote to the owner and told him she'd buy it.

During the years when she worked in Cambridge for the Physical Science Study Committee, Berenice began having the necessary repairs done on the old house. Once it had been made comfortable, she planned to start spending her summers in the

Abbott settled in Blanchard, Maine, in 1966 after purchasing a former inn that once provided lodging and food to stagecoach passengers. (PHOTOGRAPH BY HANK O'NEAL)

Blanchard house to take refuge from steamy New York. In her sixties now, she even began to think about making it her retirement home.

Elizabeth McCausland didn't share Berenice's enthusiasm for the house or Maine itself. She was busy with her writing, teaching, and consulting work, a professional life that was centered in New York. She had no wish to leave the city. Berenice wasn't sure what to do.

Before long, however, moving out of New York became a necessity. During the late 1950s Berenice began to experience serious health problems. She couldn't walk up a flight of stairs or physically exert herself in any way without struggling for oxygen. Even eating robbed her of her breath. And she had a cough that wouldn't go away. Doctors told Berenice that she had emphysema, a disease that had done serious damage to her lungs. Years of smoking had taken their toll.

Berenice was told to quit smoking—and she did. But that wasn't enough. In 1962, she underwent surgery to remove damaged lung tissue.

Berenice was also told to give up working in her airless darkroom and seriously consider leaving New York for a place with better air. When it came to deciding where to live, the house in Maine was the obvious choice. She began gradually moving her personal belongings and darkroom equipment from her Commerce Street apartment to Blanchard.

In the midst of the changeover, tragedy struck. In the spring of 1965, death claimed Elizabeth McCausland, who had been ill with complications of diabetes. Berenice had lost the friend of a lifetime. It was a terrible blow to her.

Newly settled in her Blanchard home, Berenice poses with Butch, her pet cat. (PHOTOGRAPH BY ARNOLD CRANE)

After McCausland's passing, Abbott gave up any misgivings she might have had about moving to Maine. By 1966 she was ready to embark on a new life, contentedly living in her Blanchard home, alone except for Butch, her big tomcat.

There was plenty to keep her busy. Her scientific photographs were attracting widespread attention, giving an important boost to her career. Other examples of her work, especially her New York photographs, were being exhibited frequently.

Berenice had not lived in Maine very long before she began photographing the landscapes and the people. Of the many hundreds of photographs she eventually took, 128 were gathered together for a handsome book titled *A Portrait of Maine*. Chenoweth Hall, a friend of Berenice's from New York who now lived in Maine, did the writing.

In taking the photographs for the book, Berenice, now approaching her seventies, trudged about on potato farms and through blueberry bogs, called on rough lumber camps engulfed in snow, and boarded a variety of fishing boats along the Maine coast. *A Portrait of Maine* was published in 1968.

"It's not a spectacular book or anything like that," said Berenice. "Maine isn't a spectacular state; it's a quiet state."

Once her move to Maine was complete, Abbott's vast collection of Atget's original prints, duplicate prints, and negative glass plates became a problem for her. When the Atget material was stored in the Commerce Street building, which happened to be fireproof, Berenice seldom worried about it. Keeping the collection in the old clapboard house in Maine was a different story.

Abbott began seeking a museum or other cultural institution that would serve as a permanent home for the collection. In 1968, after a long period of negotiation, New York's Museum of Modern Art agreed to purchase it. Berenice was to receive fifty thousand dollars, although she didn't get to keep the full amount. Julien Levy got what Berenice called "a big chunk" of that amount, per their agreement of 1930.

Berenice never felt the Museum of Modern Art treated her fairly in the transaction, believing that the collection was worth

A charming house in Belfast, Maine, a row of mailboxes, and an age-old tree were the chief ingredients in this skillfully composed Abbott photograph.
(COMMERCE GRAPHICS LTD., INC.)

much more than the amount she received. Something else bothered her. A museum official promised Berenice that the Atget prints and negatives would be known as the Abbott Collection. She later learned the museum called it the Abbott-Levy Collection. Berenice felt betrayed.

At the time that Berenice was seeking to find a home for the Atget material and concentrating on her various publishing projects, the world of fine photography was being recast. More and more collectors were beginning to look upon photographs as "real" art, in the same category as paintings, sculpture, and drawings. Museums were paying much more attention to photographs. Galleries that put the work of photographers up for sale were opening. Art auction houses started holding regular public sales in which fine photographs were being sold to the highest bidders. The changes were to transform Berenice's life and that of virtually every other photographer of renown. Many were to become superstars.

Lee Witkin, a thirty-four-year-old magazine writer, photographer, and editor, was in the forefront of what was taking place. An ardent collector of fine arts, Witkin bought what pleased him, mostly etchings and oil paintings. When he decided in 1969 to open his own tiny gallery on East Sixtieth Street in New York, he realized that paintings were too expensive to purchase. Photographs were different. He found that he could buy the work of the very best photographers of the time for very little money.

At Witkin's first show, prints sold for fifteen to twenty-five dollars, but quickly the demand increased and Witkin kept raising the prices. Within three months the gallery was profitable. "I couldn't believe it," Witkin said.

Berenice agreed to provide Witkin with fifty prints she had made from her Atget negatives for a show at Witkin's gallery in May that year. A remarkable number sold and, as Witkin expressed it, set a pace for the gallery's future.

Witkin deeply admired Berenice. He called her "a remarkable human being—a survivor and an artist of the first rank." Witkin presented a show devoted to Berenice's photographs in September 1973. The show was divided into three parts: the Paris portraits of writers and artists of the 1920s, the photographs of New York, and what *The New York Times* described as "the handsome modernistic designs made by photographing various scientific demonstrations."

Hank O'Neal attended that show. Like most galleries, Witkin's used a system of putting a small red dot, about the size of a child's fingernail, next to any item that had been purchased. O'Neal noticed that one of Abbott's photographs, a picture of New York's financial district, had a whole string of dots next to it. A dozen or so copies of the image had already been sold.

O'Neal looked at the long line of red dots in wonder. "I realized then," he said, "how much things had changed."

11

A WOMAN OF MAINE

The booming market for fine photography helped to make a big difference in Berenice's life. From her now neatly tended, red-roofed home in Blanchard, she looked upon what was taking place with great pleasure and satisfaction.

The requests for prints of her photographs went beyond anything she had ever imagined. Museums that not long before had ignored or even rejected her now came knocking at her door. Gallery owners and private dealers clamored for her work. Letters arrived from every corner of the globe with photograph requests.

There was no need to take new photographs. Her mission now was to furnish prints of her earlier photographs, particularly her New York views, to those who wanted them.

What was happening didn't occur entirely by accident. To some extent it was propelled by Harry Lunn, an international art dealer who had become an important force in the market for fine photographs. After a career as an intelligence agent for the CIA, the enthusiastic Lunn opened an art gallery in Washington to deal in original etchings and lithographs. He became interested in fine photography in the early 1970s.

As he had done with other photographers, Lunn bought sig-

Abbott relaxes on the back porch of her Blanchard home.
(PHOTOGRAPH BY HANK O'NEAL)

nificant numbers of Abbott's prints. These he resold privately through his Washington gallery or in partnership with the Marlborough Gallery in New York. Abbott and Lunn formed a friendship that would last for the rest of her life.

Now free of financial worries, Berenice could pursue other interests. She enjoyed reading, mostly history and biography. For relaxation and exercise she took long walks and became reasonably skilled at table tennis. Sometimes she played Parcheesi, a board

Parcheesi was one of Abbott's leisure-time activities. Harry Lunn, an international dealer in art and photographs, is her opponent here. (PHOTOGRAPH BY HANK O'NEAL)

game similar to backgammon, with neighbors or visiting friends. She kept in contact with several friends from earlier times, particularly poet and novelist Djuna Barnes and artist Thelma Wood. She also took pleasure in good clothes; good food; her pet cat, Butch; and in the evening a glass or two of beer.

Berenice was both unwilling and unable to run the big house and tend to the demands of her professional life without help. Someone to do the housecleaning, buy food, and prepare meals was vital to her. But she had difficulty finding and keeping good help. She could be cranky at times, a failing she admitted to. "There's always this problem," she said. "They [her assistants] have to live in the house, and, you know, I get on their nerves and they get on mine after all." Berenice had a long string of housekeepers and darkroom assistants.

The demand for prints of her photographs was such that Berenice was often in critical need of darkroom help. She settled on Todd Watts, a New York photographer, artist, and highly skilled printer. Watts worked in Berenice's Blanchard darkroom, printing to her specifications.

Berenice eventually had a cottage built for herself on three-mile-long, crystal-clear Lake Hebron in the small town of Monson, only a few miles from Blanchard. Monson's main street had but three stores. Berenice reigned as the town's oldest citizen. As such, she was the holder of the town's ancient walking stick, the Boston Post Cane.

The new house looked like a log cabin, but inside it was stylish and comfortable. Berenice continued to use the big house for guests and as a workplace.

Events important to Berenice led her to travel from her Maine home several times a year. She made trips to Ohio to visit her mother and her sister, Hazel, though by the mid-1970s both had died. She returned to New York late in 1970 for a major event, a handsome exhibition of her photographs at the Museum of Modern Art, arranged by John Szarkowski, director of photography. The show was held in the museum's Steichen Galleries, named for her one-time antagonist, which surely must have added to her pleasure.

As Berenice entered her eighties, she gained even greater fame. In 1981 the International Center of Photography in New York teamed with the National Museum of American Art to present a major exhibition of her photos.

In 1982 the Witkin Gallery offered an exhibition of ninety of her photographs. The show was held in connection with the publication of Hank O'Neal's biography of her, titled *Berenice Abbott: American Photographer*. A caring and comprehensive account of her life and career, it offered more than 250 of Abbott's photographs and has remained the foremost book about Berenice since its publication.

During these years, Berenice received honorary degrees from Bowdoin College, Smith College, the New School for Social Research, and Ohio State University. She was inducted into the Order of Arts and Letters by the French government, becoming the first American woman to be so honored.

"I don't work anymore," Berenice, at eighty-five, told an interviewer for *The New York Times*. "I didn't like the last things I did. People should know when to quit. Now, I'm a retired hermit."

In 1985, at the age of eighty-seven, Abbott, did, in fact, make

In the spring of 1977, Abbott traveled to New York with her camera. Federal Hall on Wall Street is one of the sites she visited. (PHOTOGRAPH BY HANK O'NEAL)

a serious move toward becoming, if not entirely a hermit, at least unequivocally retired. She agreed to sell her enormous accumulation of negatives and photographs to Ronald A. Kurtz, a New Jersey aerospace metals executive. Kurtz and the company that he formed, Commerce Graphics (named for the New York street on which Berenice had lived for many years), also obtained the rights—that is, the legal ownership—to the entire body of Berenice's work.

In the years after he acquired her work, Kurtz donated sizable selections of her photographs to a good number of universities and cultural institutions, including New York's Metropolitan Museum and Museum of Modern Art, the New York Public Library, and the San Francisco Museum of Modern Art. In addition, Commerce Graphics cooperated with several cultural institutions and art galleries in providing Abbott photographs for exhibitions.

Berenice enjoyed occasional visits from her friends throughout her decades in Maine. It was not an easy journey for them. In winter the weather could be brutal. The roads became clogged with snow and impassable. But even in summer the trip was a chore. After the flight to Bangor, Maine, visitors drove fifty miles to the north and west up the Moosehead Trail through long stretches of thickly forested hills to reach Berenice's home.

The sound of an approaching automobile alerted Berenice, and often she greeted visitors in the front yard. Inside, where some of the rooms were decorated with poster-size enlargements of her favorite photographs, a wood fire might be burning, even in July or August.

Berenice made it clear to friends that she had no regrets about leaving New York and settling in Maine. "In the city you have more sophistication. So what? You miss the good things there—the good air, water, sleep.

"I wouldn't want anything different than it is now. This is a nice way to end your life."

12

AMERICAN MASTER

Early on a crisp October morning in 1989, ninety-one-year-old Berenice Abbott set out in her silver Audi from her snug cabin in Monson, Maine, on the long trek to New York City. Susan Blatchford, a neighbor and close friend who watched over Berenice in her final years, serving as her companion and caregiver, did the driving.

What drew Berenice from the solitude of the piney woods was an unprecedented exhibition of her work at the New York Public Library that celebrated her sixty-year career in photography. Organized by Julia van Haaften, curator of the library's photography collection, the show presented almost two hundred of Berenice's photographs plus material in glass cases representing the chief phases of her career. A big banner over the library's front entrance on Fifth Avenue saluted Berenice and the exhibition.

On the opening night of the show, Berenice, smallish and frail, in a black pantsuit and a sable jacket, smiled and greeted friends and admirers as she slowly eased her way through the crowded aisles of the exhibition hall lined with her framed images, many of which were now regarded as classics.

Titled "Berenice Abbott, Photographer: A Modern Vision," the

146

A huge banner saluted Abbott and the exhibition of her photographs at the New York Public Library in October 1989. (NEW YORK PUBLIC LIBRARY)

exhibition was, in a way, a walk through her life in photography. There were her portraits of the leading figures of the Paris art world in the 1920s—James Joyce, Djuna Barnes, Jean Cocteau, and Eugène Atget. There were the New York City images from the 1930s—the bridges, towering buildings, storefronts, and bustling streets. There were her scientific photographs—the bouncing balls, soap bubbles, and spinning wrench.

Some of Berenice's inventions were also on exhibit. These included the canvas photographer's carryall jacket and her unipod, a long-legged camera stand. Her many books were assembled in other display cases.

There were examples of Atget's work, too, a salute to Berenice's almost single-handed struggle to win recognition for the French photographer.

It was an evening of triumph for Berenice. "It was very crowded, and I didn't get a chance to speak to her," recalled Todd Watts. "But once during the evening, she looked at me with a knowing grin. It was if she was saying that it was her night. She was the star, and she loved it."

After attending the exhibition, Berenice returned to her home in Maine. She quietly lived there until her death from congestive heart failure two years later. She was ninety-three years old when she died on December 10, 1991.

In the years following her passing, Berenice's many accomplishments in photography continued to be recognized. In 1998 the University of Maine Museum of Art exhibited many of the photographs taken by Berenice on her 1954 roundtrip from Fort Kent, Maine, to Key West, Florida. One of the museum's best-attended shows in years, it also toured Maine schools. In 2004 the same museum presented an exhibition of Abbott and Atget photos titled "Cities' Portraits."

Abbott's New York photographs received another and unusual expression of tribute in 2005 with the publication of *New York Changing: Revisiting Berenice Abbott's New York*. The handsome book was the work of Douglas Levere, a New York–based photographer. Over a period of six years Levere had returned to more than one hundred of Abbott's original sites and re-photographed them at the same time of day and year, using the same type of camera and lenses that she had used.

Abbott's view of oyster houses at South Street and Pike Slip in Manhattan, photographed in 1937, was rephotographed by Douglas Levere in 2002. (COMMERCE GRAPHICS LTD., INC./MUSEUM OF THE CITY OF NEW YORK)

Levere's photographs show clearly how New York had changed since the 1930s. But more than that, as architectural critic Paul Goldberger pointed out in a foreword to the book, Levere "paid the greatest homage imaginable" to Abbott and her pictures. In addition, said Goldberger, Levere underscored the timelessness of Abbott's photographs by connecting her work to the city as it existed in the early years of the twenty-first century.

During the 1980s and 1990s, much of photography started to become highly personal and fanciful. Some photographers transformed the appearance of an image to create a mood or visual impression, much as the pictorialists had done years before. They might combine two or more negatives into a single print or use their photographs for the basis of painted images. Other photographers staged scenes for the camera.

Fanciful photography was given a boost by the introduction of computer technology and digitalization in the late 1980s. With picture-editing software, a photograph can be altered in countless ways. It can be lightened, darkened, or cropped. Defects can be removed. Parts of one image can be merged with another. Text can be included. With drawing tools, lines and brush strokes can be added.

Of course, any photograph with an unreal or manipulated quality would be scorned by Berenice. "Sheer escapism" is the way she once described such work. "It doesn't amount to a row of beans," she once said. "[The photographers] don't know themselves what they mean, don't know what they're saying or doing."

She never liked the idea of photographers using their work as a means of self-expression. "You're not projecting your emotions

Taken on July 17, 1991, her ninety-third birthday, this was Berenice Abbott's last portrait. (Photograph by Hank O'Neal)

onto a two-dimensional sheet of paper," she said. "Who cares about your emotions except you?"

She would have been pleased that the digital means of creating photographs did not entirely lessen people's interest in realism. Documentary-style photographs are obvious in news pictures and also those that relate to poverty, homelessness, the environment, or other topics common to the social landscape.

During her lifetime, Abbott saw photography evolve from a modest family pastime to a central feature of American culture, gaining worldwide acceptance as an art form. Through the decades, in the face of numerous cults and fads and an ever-increasing emphasis on individual style, Abbott's views never changed. Her one ambition was to always use the camera as honestly as possible so as to clearly and artfully document the world about her.

Whether she was photographing a person, a skyscraper, or a scientific experiment, the realistic image formed by the lens is what concerned Berenice Abbott. She photographed what was there. The image was her message. Her dedication to that principle is what enabled Abbott to create her extraordinary body of work and achieve legendary status as an absolute master of her medium.

Acknowledgments

Ronald A. Kurtz, president of Commerce Graphics, Ltd., Inc., generously supported this project almost from the beginning, supplying the scores of Abbott photographs that appear in this book, granting permission to publish quoted remarks from the lengthy James McQuaid–David Tait interview with Abbott, and providing information and insight about Abbott, her friends, and those she worked with. I am deeply grateful to him. Cindy Johnson, director of Commerce Graphics, and Natalie Evans were also very helpful.

Special thanks are also due Bonnie Yochelson, former curator of Prints and Photographs at the Museum of the City of New York and author of *Berenice Abbott: Changing New York,* for providing me with vital background information about Abbott and for reading the manuscript to help assure freedom from error. Hank O'Neal, a long-time friend of Abbott's and author of *Berenice Abbott: American Photographer,* shared his memories of Abbott with me, provided several of his Abbott photographs for use, and also vetted the manuscript. Peter Barr was another who shared his insights with me, these derived from his experience in preparing his doctoral dissertation, "On Becoming Documentary: Berenice's Abbott's Photographs, 1925–1939."

I'm also grateful for the assistance I received in working at various archives, particularly from Bob Shamis, curator of Prints and Photographs, Museum of the City of New York; Carmen Hendershott, reference librarian, New School University; Pamela Reed Sanchez, George Eastman House, International Center of Photography; Julia van Haaften, David Lowe, and Jim Moske, New York Public Library; and Joy Weiner, Archives of American Art.

Special thanks are also due a number of individuals who were generous with their time in providing me with specific information about Abbott, including Evelynne Z. Daitz, the Witkin Gallery; Howard Daitz; Todd Watts; Robert Feldman, Parasol Press; Denise Bethel, Sotheby's; and Carole Heinlein of Calais, Maine. Daile Kaplan, Swann Galleries, and Sal Alberti and James Lowe, James Lowe Autographs, also provided valuable help.

Jennifer B. Greene, my editor at Clarion Books, championed this project from its earliest days and applied her considerable editorial expertise in shaping and enhancing the manuscript. Thank you, Jennifer.

Notes

References in this section are to books and articles cited in the Bibliography, beginning on page 161, unless otherwise noted.

Introduction

O'Neal, "the finest record ever made of an American city," is from O'Neal, 1982, p. 16.

Abbott, "a pioneer of modern photography," is from Hagen, p. D25.

Abbott, "to communicate the realities of life," is from Abbott, 1953, p. 12.

Abbott, "precious" and "exclusive," is from Worswick, p. 34.

Abbott, "advanced or super-pictorialist school," is from Worswick, p. 34.

"Special artistry," "extraordinary eye," and "master photographer" are from Kramer, 1970, p. 58.

Chapter 1: Spirit of a Rebel

Abbott, "The last thing in the world," is quoted in McQuaid and Tait, p. 4.

Abbott, "I was about five," is quoted in McQuaid and Tait, p. 6.

Abbott, "'Oh, Berenice, you have a new papa,'" is quoted in McQuaid and Tait, p. 6.

Abbott, "I don't really like to talk about it," is quoted in McQuaid and Tait, p. 8.

Abbott, "just a madman," is quoted in McQuaid and Tait, p. 4.

Abbott, "I think [it was] to get away," is quoted in McQuaid and Tait, p. 8.

Abbott, "I got hard pretty early," is quoted in McQuaid and Tait, p. 12.

Abbott, "a very independent kid," is from Mitchell, p. 12.

Abbott, "Marriage is the finish of women," is from Berman, p. 89.

Abbott, "first act of rebellion" and "The day after I graduated," are quoted in Abbott's autobiographical sketch, 1954 (unpaged).

Abbott, "My bobbed hair startled the campus," is quoted in Abbott's autobiographical sketch, 1954.

Dialogue, "I think there is something I should tell you," is quoted in Mc-Quaid and Tait, p. 36.

Abbott, "I just thought history was the dullest thing on earth," is quoted in McQuaid and Tait, p. 27.

Abbott, "[A] lot of stupidity flourishes," is quoted in McQuaid and Tait, p. 30.

Abbott, "I think what she wanted," is quoted in McQuaid and Tait, pp. 31, 32.

Abbott, "It wasn't easy," is quoted in McQuaid and Tait, 1975, p. 41.

Abbott, "pull," is quoted in Abbott's autobiographical sketch, 1954.

Coleman, "unsettling" and "[N]o single clue," are from Coleman, p. 22.

CHAPTER 2: THE VILLAGE

"An independent republic" and "socialism, sex, poetry" are from *Frommer's* online, last accessed on December 7, 2005, at www.frommers.com/destinations/newyorkcity/0021020033.hmtl.

Abbott, "the youngest thing around," is from Abbott's autobiographical sketch, 1954.

Abbott, "He was just what I needed," is quoted in McQuaid and Tait, p. 50.

Abbott, "seemed like the hell of a sausage factory," is from Mitchell, p. 12.

Abbott, "just to earn a buck" and "nightmare," are from McQuaid and Tait, p. 58.

Abbott, "This will get you over it," is quoted in McQuaid and Tait, p. 46.

Abbott, "very cheap rent," is quoted from Abbott's autobiographical sketch, 1954.

"Dirty bourgeois" is quoted in McQuaid and Tait, p. 57.

Abbott, "There were a lot of kids," is quoted in McQuaid and Tait, p. 49.

Abbott, "far out," "weird values," and "was a form of rebellion," is quoted in McQuaid and Tait, pp. 62, 63.

Steiner, "I used to meet her at parties," is from Zwingle, p. 57.

Abbott, "When she read her poems," is quoted from Abbott's autobiographical sketch, 1954.

Abbott, "every whim and fancy," is quoted from McQuaid and Tait, p. 57.

Abbott, "She criticized their work honestly," is quoted from Abbott's biographical sketch, 1954.

Hartmann, "my art children," is quoted from the Introduction to The Life and Times of Sadakichi Hartmann, 1867–1944, An Exhibition Presented and Co-sponsored by the University Library and the Riverside Press-Enterprise Co. at the University of California, Riverside, May 1–May 31, 1970.

Hartmann, "You become somebody!" is from remarks delivered by Bernard Cohen at the Berenice Abbott memorial service, New York Public Library, February 8, 1992.

CHAPTER 3: PARIS

Abbott, "We were completely liberated," is from Russell, p. 70.

Abbott, "Somehow, fantastically enough," is from Abbott's autobiographical sketch, 1954.

Abbott, "He was wealthy and we would go out in the evening," is from Mc-Quaid and Tait, p. 128.

Abbott, "as one of the most valuable attributes," is from Abbott's autobiographical sketch, 1954.

Dialogue, "My brain clicked at that moment," is from Abbott's autobiographical sketch, 1954.

Abbott, "Sister, you have to make this go," is quoted in McQuaid and Tait, p. 143.

Abbott, "Man Ray was amazed," is from Abbott's autobiographical sketch, 1954.

Abbott, "The first [portraits] I took," is from O'Neal, 1982, p. 10.

Abbott, "He changed my whole life," is from O'Neal, 1982, p. 10.

Abbott, "His portraits of men were good," is from Berman, p. 89.

Abbott, "To photograph a person," and "I was ready," are from Barr, p. 44.

"A photographer for the time being," is from "A Landmark Portraitist for an Extraordinary Age," The New York Times, April 14, 1995, p. C1.

Kramer, "[The portraits] sum up," is from "The Entertaining Nadar, A Pioneer in Photography," New York Observer, April 24, 1995, pp. 1, 21.

New York Herald of Paris, "There is absolutely no striving," is quoted in Barr, p. 46.

Chapter 4: "A Magical Record"

Abbott, "the most beautiful photographs ever made," is from Berman, p. 91.

"A magical record," is from "Paris and Its Soul: A Magical Record," *The New York Times,* Jun 30, 1929, p. SM7.

Abbott, "slightly stooped . . . tired, sad," is from Abbott, *The World of Atget,* p. viii.

Abbott, "The subjects were not sensational," is from Abbott, *The World of Atget,* p. viii.

Abbott, "I had always seen him in patched work clothes," is from Berman, p. 91.

Abbott, "his and mine," is from O'Neal, p. 12.

Beach, "the official portraitist of 'the Crowd,'" is quoted in Beach, pp. 111–12.

Abbott, "what particular theme or subject of American life," is quoted from Barr, p. 6.

Abbott, "an extremely strong pull," is quoted in McQuaid and Tate, p. 247.

Abbott, "The American scene just fascinated me," is quoted in McQuaid and Tait, pp. 238–39.

Abbott, "Find a worthy subject," is from Berman, p. 92.

Chapter 5: A New Beginning

Abbott, "I realized from my early days," is quoted in McQuaid and Tait, p. 657.

Abbott, "went out the window," is from McQuaid and Tate, p. 247.

Stieglitz, "I have a vision of life," is quoted in Boxer, p. E31.

Evans, "disastrous on both sides," is from Hambourg and Phillips, p. 47.

Chapter 6: "A Big Theme"

Abbott, "Just notes," is quoted in Yochelson, p. 13.

Abbott, "I was shy about setting up my camera," is from Marks, p. 157.

Abbott, "I wasn't smart," is from Berman, p. 92.

▼

Abbott, "Women did not wear slacks then," is from Shepard, "Berenice Abbott," p. C17.

Abbott, "Old New York is fast disappearing," is from O'Neal, 1982, p. 16.

"Miles and miles of such pictures" is quoted from Yochelson, p. 18.

McCausland, "a big theme," is quoted from Yochelson, p. 19.

McCausland, "sympathetic warmth and understanding," is from McCausland, 1935, p. 15.

Abbott, "the first intelligent," is from Yochelson, 1997, note 36, p. 33.

Abbott, "to capture the spirit of the metropolis," is from O'Neal, 1982, p. 17.

Abbott, "her beautiful brain," is quoted in McQuaid and Tait, p. 427.

Abbott, "We used to argue about that," is quoted in McQuaid and Tait, p. 427.

Abbott, "The best friend I ever had," is quoted in McQuaid and Tait, p. 430.

Abbott, "to stick a camera in the face of someone," is from O'Neal, 1982, p. 17.

McCausland, "a portrait in words and photographs," is quoted in Yochelson, p. 20.

CHAPTER 7: PICTURES OF A CHANGING CITY

Dialogue, "Now listen," and "I'm not a nice girl!" are from O'Neal, 1982, p. 18.

Abbott, "They thought you wanted to commit suicide," is from O'Neal, 1982, p. 4.

Abbott, "The man [in the photo]," is from O'Neal, 1982, p. 167.

Abbott, "I had devised a very low tripod," is from O'Neal, 1982, p. 130.

Abbott, "You want to take a subway rush," is from Marks, p. 169.

Abbott, "Cameras are primitive today," is from Marks, p. 169.

van Vechten, "I went to see your New York pictures," is from O'Neal, 1982, p. 28.

Newhall, "represents the best," is quoted in Yochelson, p. 31.

CHAPTER 8: TEACHER, AUTHOR, INVENTOR

Abbott, "I'd probably faint and have to be carried out," is quoted in McQuaid and Tait, p. 266.

Abbott, "The most terrifying thing I ever did," is quoted in McQuaid and Tait, p. 266.

"Such tasks as a professional photographer meets" is quoted in *The New School Bulletin, 1949–1950,* Vol. 76, No. 1, September 5, 1949, p. 160.

Abbott, "There were a few talented students," is from O'Neal, 1982, p. 18.

Abbott, "devious manipulation," is from Abbott, *New Guide,* p. 7.

Abbott, quoting Emerson, "Avoid prettiness," is from Abbott, *New Guide,* p. 7.

Abbott, "Photography is to communicate," is from Abbott, *New Guide,* p. 12.

Abbott, "We live in a world," is from O'Neal, 1982, p. 20.

Abbott, "a flea attacking a giant," is from O'Neal, *The Beauty of Physics,* p. 3.

Abbott, "For two years," is from O'Neal, 1982, p. 21.

CHAPTER 9: FOCUSING ON SCIENCE

Abbott, "Steichen is an example," is from Berman, p. 87.

Steichen, "Intuition is simply keen perception," is from Gee, 1980–81, p. 8.

Abbott, "My knees were sort of quaking," is quoted in McQuaid and Tait, p. 616.

Abbott, "The greatest influence," is quoted in O'Neal, p. 24.

Abbott, "They were what I can only call," is from Worswick, p. 34.

"Out of the swim" is from Gee, 1997, p. 217.

Abbott, "If you went up," is quoted in McQuaid and Tait, p. 509.

"It can truly be said" is quoted in Gee, 1980–81, p. 5.

Dr. E. P. Little, "This is just what we want," is quoted in O'Neal, p. 27.

Abbott, "They got me out," is from Russell, p. 70.

O'Neal, "[The science photographs] not only present the laws of physics . . ." is from O'Neal, *The Beauty of Physics,* p. 11.

Chapter 10: An Awakening Interest

Abbott, "I liked it better," is quoted in McQuaid and Tait, p. 469.

Abbott, "crazy about Maine," is quoted in McQuaid and Tait, p. 427.

Abbott, "It's not a spectacular book," is quoted in McQuaid and Tait, p. 475.

Witkin, "I couldn't believe it," is from Mezey, p. 174.

Witkin, "a remarkable human being," is quoted in Witkin, 1979, p. 116.

"The handsome modernistic designs" is from Thornton, 1973, p. 156.

O'Neal, "I realized then," is from my interview of him.

Chapter 11: A Woman of Maine

Abbott, "There's always this problem," is quoted in McQuaid and Tait, p. 66.

Abbott, "I don't work any more," is from "New York Day by Day," *The New York Times,* March 8, 1964, p. B3.

Abbott, "In the city you have," is from *American Photographer,* Zwingle, p. 67.

Chapter 12: American Master

Watts, "It was very crowded," is from my interview of him.

Goldberger, "paid the greatest homage imaginable," is from Levere, 2005, p. 8.

Abbott, "Sheer escapism," is from Franklin, p. 20.

Abbott, "You're not projecting your emotions," is from Franklin, p. 20.

BIBLIOGRAPHY

BOOKS BY AND ABOUT BERENICE ABBOTT

Abbott, Berenice. Autobiographical Sketch. This untitled and unpaged sketch, dated February 5, 1954, and covering the period from 1917 to 1925, in the McCausland Papers on deposit at the Archives of American Art, Smithsonian Institution, New York City.

———. *Berenice Abbott: Photographs.* With a foreword by Muriel Rukeyser and an introduction by David Vestal. Washington: Smithsonian Institution Press, 1990.

———. *A Guide to Better Photography.* New York: Crown Publishers, 1941.

———. *New Guide to Better Photography.* New York: Crown Publishers, 1953.

———. *A Portrait of Maine,* text by Chenoweth Hall. New York: Macmillan, 1968.

———. *The View Camera Made Simple.* Chicago: Ziff-Davis, 1948.

———. *The World of Atget.* New York: Horizon, 1964.

———, and Henry-Russell Hitchcock. *Constructing Modernism* (an updated version of the catalog for the 1934 exhibition). Middletown, Conn.: Davison Art Center, Wesleyan University, 1993.

Berenice Abbott, with an essay by Julia van Haaften. New York: Aperture Foundation, 1988.

Lanier, Henry Wysham. *Greenwich Village, Today and Yesterday.* Photographs by Berenice Abbott. New York: Harper & Brothers, 1949.

McCausland, Elizabeth. *Berenice Abbott: Changing New York.* Photographs by Berenice Abbott. New York: E. P. Dutton, 1939.

———. *New York in the Thirties as Photographed by Berenice Abbott* (a reprint of *Berenice Abbott: Changing New York,* published in 1939). New York: Dover Publications, 1973.

O'Neal, Hank. *The Beauty of Physics.* Photographs by Berenice Abbott. New York: Academy of Sciences, 1987 (catalog of the exhibition, January 30–March 27, 1987).

Sotheby's. *Berenice Abbott's New York: Photographs from the Museum of the City of New York* (catalog for the auction, October 23, 2002).

Tousley, Nancy. *The Berenice Abbott Portfolios.* Calgary, Alberta: Glenbow Museum, 1982 (catalog of the exhibition, April 24–May 31, 1982).

Valens, Evans. *The Attractive Universe: Gravity and the Shape of Space.* Photographs by Berenice Abbott. Cleveland: World Publishing Co., 1969.

———. *Magnet.* Photographs by Berenice Abbott. Cleveland: World Publishing Co, 1964.

———. *Motion.* Photographs by Berenice Abbott. Cleveland: World Publishing Co., 1965.

Worswick, Clark. *Berenice Abbott & Eugène Atget* (with text by Berenice Abbott from *The World of Atget,* published in 1964). Santa Fe, N.M.: Arena Editions, 2002.

BOOKS AND ARTICLES

Baldwin, Gordon. *Looking at Photographs: A Guide to Technical Terms*. Malibu, Calif.: J. Paul Getty Museum, 1991.

Barnet, Andrea. *All-Night Party: The Women of Bohemian Greenwich Village and Harlem, 1913-1930*. Chapel Hill, N.C: Algonquin Books, 2004.

Barr, Peter. *Becoming Documentary: Berenice Abbott's Photographs, 1925–1939*. (Doctoral dissertation.) Boston: Boston University, 1997.

Beach, Sylvia. *Shakespeare and Company*. Lincoln, Neb.: University of Nebraska Press, 1991 (reprint of New York: Harcourt, Brace, 1959 edition).

Berman, Avis. "The Unflinching Eye of Berenice Abbott." *ARTnews*, January 1981, pp. 86–93.

Boxer, Sarah. "The Evolution of Alfred Stieglitz, Ever the Perfectionist." *The New York Times*, August 2, 2002, p. E31.

———. "A Legacy That Crossed the Ocean." *The New York Times*, October 4, 1996, p. C27.

Carlton, Sarah. "Berenice Abbott." *American Girl*, August 1931, pp. 12–13, 35–36.

Coleman. A. D. "Career of Illustrious Photographer Enshrined at Library." *The New York Observer*, October 23, 1989, p. 22.

Franklin, Lynn. *Profiles of Maine*. Waldoboro, Maine: *Maine Antique Digest*, 1976.

Gee, Helen. *Limelight: A Greenwich Village Photography Gallery and Coffeehouse in the Fifties*. Albuquerque, N.M.: University of New Mexico Press, 1997.

———. *Photography of the Fifties: An American Perspective.* Tucson, Ariz.: The University of Arizona, 1980–81.

Grundberg, Andy. "Images of an Optimistic, Self-Assured Past." *The New York Times,* October 15, 1989, p. H37.

———. "In New York City, Berenice Abbott Found Her Best Subject." *The New York Times,* December 12, 1982, p. H37.

Hagen, Charles. "Berenice Abbott, 93, Dies; Her Photographs Captured New York in Transition." *The New York Times,* December 11, 1991, p. D25.

Hambourg, Maria Morris, and Christopher Phillips. *The New Vision: Photography Between the World Wars: Ford Motor Company Collection at the Metropolitan Museum of Art.* New York: The Metropolitan Museum of Art, 1989.

Hawes, Elizabeth. "Berenice Abbott." *Mirabella,* March 1990, pp. 73–77.

Herenden, Anne. "Paris and Its Soul: A Magical Record." *The New York Times,* June 30, 1929, p. TK.

Kramer, Hilton. "The Entertaining Nadar, A Long-lived Pioneer in French Photography." *The New Observer,* April 24, 1995, pp. 1, 21.

———. "Miss Abbott: 63 Photos at the Modern." *The New York Times,* December 11, 1970, p. 58.

———. "Vanished City Life by Berenice Abbott on View." *The New York Times,* November 27, 1981, p. C1.

Marks, Robert W. "Chronicler of Our Times." *Coronet,* December 1938, pp. 157–169.

McCausland, Elizabeth. "The Photography of Berenice Abbott." *Trend*, March-April 1935, pp. 15–21.

Mezey, Alexandra. "Selling Photography as Art Put Lee Witkin in the Picture." *People*, April 9, 1979, pp. 75–77.

Mitchell, Margaretta K. *Recollections: Ten Women of Photography.* New York: The Viking Press, 1979.

Newman, Julia. "Berenice Abbott, Pioneer: Past and Present." *U.S. Camera*, February 1960, pp. 34–39, 112.

O'Neal, Hank. *Berenice Abbott: American Photographer,* introduction by John Canaday; commentary by Berenice Abbott. New York: McGraw-Hill, 1982.

Russell, John. "Her Camera Now Depicts Still Life in Maine." *The New York Times,* November 16, 1980, p. 70.

van Haaftan, Julia, ed. *Berenice Abbott, Photographer: A Modern Vision.* A selection of photographs and essays. New York: New York Public Library, 1989.

Shepard, Richard F. "Photographer Abbott: A Vision of New York." *The International Herald-Tribune,* October 6, 1989.

———. "Berenice Abbott: Still Feisty and Eager at 91." *The New York Times,* October 4, 1989, p. C17.

Thornton, Gene. "Berenice Abbott: She Is Decisive." *The New York Times,* September 16, 1973, p. 156.

Witkin, Lee D. *A Ten Year Salute: A Selection of Photographs in Celebration of the Witkin Gallery,* 1969–1979. Danbury, N.H.: Addison House, 1979.

————, and Barbara London. *The Photograph Collector's Guide*. Boston: New York Graphic Society, 1979.

Yochelson, Bonnie, ed.. *Berenice Abbott: Changing New York*. New York: New Press, Museum of the City of New York, 1997.

————. *New York Changing: Revisiting Berenice Abbott's New York*. Photographs by Douglas Levere. New York: Princeton Architectural Press, 2005.

Zwingle, Erla. "A Life of Her Own." *American Photographer*, April 1986, pp. 54–67.

OTHER SOURCES

Berenice Abbott: A View of the 20th Century. Los Angeles, Ishtar Films, 1992. Filmed during her ninety-first and ninety-second years, this 57-minute video offers a survey of Abbott's life and work, with frequent and straightforward comments from Abbott herself.

McQuaid, James, and David Tait. "Interview with Berenice Abbott," a 663-page transcript of question-and-answer sessions conducted by McQuaid and Tait at Abbott's home in Maine in July 1975. The property of Commerce Graphics Ltd., Inc., the transcript is on deposit at the International Museum of Photography at George Eastman House, Rochester, New York.

The New York Public Library's online gallery of photographs, prints, maps, and other holdings (http://digitalgallery.nypl.org) offers 343 photographs from "Changing New York," Abbott's project to document New York City in the 1930s. Each entry includes the title of the photograph, the date it was taken, its size, and other physical characteristics.

Interview with Hank O'Neal by the author, June 22, 2004.

Interview with Todd Watts by the author, August 26, 2004.

Index

Note: Page numbers in **bold** type refer to illustrations.